D1566867

The Sudbury Valley School Experience

with photographs by
Andrew Brilliant and Carol Palmer

Sudbury Valley School Press
2 Winch Street
Framingham, MA 01701

Contents

Introduction

The time was 1967. A small group of parents living in the Greater Framingham area had been hunting all over the country for a school that met our requirements. We had travelled far and wide, visited and read about all sorts of places -- and had come up empty-handed.

The main thing we all had in common was a deep conviction that the existing educational system would do our children irreparable harm. We felt we had to do whatever was necessary to provide the kind of environment we wished our children to have.

So it was that Sudbury Valley School was founded in 1968.

The starting point for all our thinking was the apparently revolutionary idea that a child is a person, worthy of full respect as a human being. These are simple words with devastatingly complex consequences, chief of which is that the child's agenda for its own life is as important as anyone else's agenda -- parents, family, friends, or even the community. In the school we wanted for our children, their inner needs would have to be given priority in their education at every point.

As a practical matter, this meant that our children's activities at school would have to be launched on their own initiative. There could be

no externally imposed curriculum, no arbitrary
requirements dictating what they should do with
themselves. The school had to be a nurturing
environment in which the children themselves
schedule their time, choose what they wish to do.

Personal respect also had to be the foundation of our children's process of socialization.
This led us directly to the concept of democracy
as an institutional imperative. Democracy alone
is built on the solid foundation of equal respect
for all members of the community, and for their
ideas and hopes. And so it became a cornerstone
of our philosophy to give everyone at school,
without exception, a full and equal voice in
running the school.

An interesting feature of this respect
extended to all members of the school community
had to do with out attitude toward parents. So
many educators viewed parents as a nuisance at
best, a downright menace at worst. This did not
seem right to us, mostly because we were founding
a school primarily as parents! Any way we looked
at it, parents definitely had a place in children's education. From the beginning, we held to
this belief, and structured the school
accordingly.

This book is a collection of selected essays
and short pieces written about the school over the
years. They were chosen for their relevance to
the current school scene, and for their ability to
convey an understanding of what Sudbury Valley
School is all about.

The book was put together in response to a
need, frequently stated by visitors, prospective
enrollees, and educators. We have often been
asked for more background material on various
aspects of the school. Although the material was

available, it was scattered through dozens of
publications, most of them issues of our News-
letter, which is published approximately eight
times a year. Some minor editorial changes have
been made in transcribing these writings from
their original sources, in order to make the
material more readable and consistent with current
school usage.

Perhaps the best way to open the book is with
an excerpt from a recent school catalog. Entitled
"A Typical Day...A Typical Year", it says:

Even after reading and hearing about the
school, and often even after visiting, many
people still wonder and ask what a "typical
day" is like at school, both for students and
for staff. It often comes as a surprise that
we have so much trouble responding to such a
question.

Our problem is twofold: first, people at
school are so different from each other, that
no two of them ever do the same thing, at
least not for long. Second, there is such
total freedom to use time that each person
often varies his activities from day to day,
or week to week, or month to month.

The variety is truly amazing -- until
you realize that in the world outside of
schools, chances are that any group of people
not pre-selected will show just as many
differences. At Sudbury Valley, we see just
about everything. One person will settle
into a perfectly predictable pattern for
months on end, always doing the same things
in the same sequence at the same times -- and
then suddenly change to another predictable
pattern. Another person will, at totally
unpredictable times, be doing something else

each time. Another person will go on a
series of short term binges -- a few intensive weeks (or months) of this, followed by a
few intensive weeks (or months) of that.

Some people play all day. Some people
talk all day. Some people paint or study or
cook all day. Some people do a little of
each of these things, according to some
schedule they have for themselves. Some come
early and leave early, some come late and
leave late. One week you are likely to find
many people at school by opening time, and a
bustling school soon after. The next week
the school may be quiet until mid-morning.

Time assumes a different aspect at
Sudbury Valley. Here there are no bells, no
periods, no terms, no grades, no "freshman,"
no "sophomores," no "juniors," no "seniors";
no "preschoolers," no "post-graduates." Time
belongs to each student in a very personal
sense. Each student learns to understand and
work with his own unique internal rhythm,
pace, and speed. No one is a fast learner,
no one a slow learner. All have in common
the quest for a personal identity that is
whole, and individual, and that, once found,
makes all reference to time seem trivial.

And that is the heart of the matter. By com-
bining absolute respect for self with a deep sense
of community, Sudbury Valley has put into practice
ideals we have long struggled for. It is the
stuff our dreams were made of, brought to life.

The Sudbury Valley School Press

Back to Basics

Daniel Greenberg

Why go to school?

For people who like to think through for themselves the important questions in life, Sudbury Valley stands as a challenge to the accepted answers.

Intellectual basics

The first phrase that pops into everyone's mind is: "We go to school to learn." That's the intellectual goal. It comes before all the others. So much so, that "getting an education " has come to mean "learning" -- a bit narrow, to be sure, but it gets the priorities clear.

Then why don't people learn more in schools today? Why all the complaints? Why the seemingly limitless expenditures just to tread water, let alone to progress?

The answer is embarrassingly simple. Schools today are institutions in which "learning" is taken to mean "being taught." You want people to learn? Teach them! You want them to learn more? Teach them more! And more! Work them harder. Drill them longer.

But learning is a process you do, not a process that is done to you! That is true of everyone. It's basic.

What makes people learn? Funny anyone should
ask. Over two thousand years ago, Aristotle
started his most important book with the univer-
sally accepted answer: "Human beings are naturally
curious." Descartes put it slightly differently,
also at the beginning of his major work: "I think,
therefore I am." Learning, thinking, actively
using your mind -- it's the essence of being
human. It's natural.

More so even than the great drives -- hunger,
thirst, sex. When you're engrossed in something
-- the key word is "engrossed" -- you forget about
all the other drives until they overwhelm you.
Even rats do that, as was shown a long time ago.

Who would think of forcing people to eat, or
drink, or have sex? (Of course, I'm not talking
about people who have a specific disability that
affects their drives; nor is anything I am writing
here about education meant to apply to people who
have specific mental impairments, which must be
dealt with in special, clinical ways.) No one
sticks people's faces in bowls of food, every hour
on the hour, to be sure they'll eat; no one
closets people with mates, eight periods a day, to
make sure they'll couple.

Does that sound ridiculous? How much more
ridiculous is it, then, to try to force people to
do that which above all else comes most naturally
to them! And everyone knows just how widespread
this overpowering curiosity is. All books on
childrearing go to great lengths to instruct
parents on how to keep their little children out
of things -- especially once they are mobile. We
don't stand around pushing our one year olds to
explore. On the contrary, we tear our hair out as
they tear our house apart, we seek ways to harness
them, imprison them in playpens. And the older

they get, the more mischief they get into. Did
you ever deal with a ten year old? A teenager?

People go to school to learn. To learn, they
must be left alone and given time. When they need
help, it should be given, if we want the learning
to proceed at its own natural pace. But make no
mistake: if a person is determined to learn, they
will overcome every obstacle and learn in spite of
everything. So you don't have to help; help just
makes the process a little quicker. Overcoming
obstacles is one of the main activities of learning. It does no harm to leave a few.

But if you bother the person, if you insist
he stop his own natural learning and do instead
what you want him to do, between 9:00 AM and 9:50,
and between 10:00 AM and 10:50 and so forth, not
only won't he learn what he has a passion to
learn, but he will also hate you, hate what you
are forcing him to do, and lose all taste for
learning, at least temporarily.

Every time you think of a class in one of
those schools out there, just imagine the teacher
was forcing spinach and milk and carrots and
sprouts (all those good things) down each student's throat with a giant ramrod.

Sudbury Valley leaves its students be.
Period. No maybes. No exceptions. We help if we
can when we are asked. We never get in the way.
People come here primarily to learn. And that's
what they all do, every day, all day.

Vocational basics

The nitty-gritty of going to school always
comes up next, after "learning." When it comes
right down to it, most people don't really give a
damn what or how much they or their children learn
at school, as long as they are able to have a

successful career -- to get a good job. That
means money, status, advancement. The better the
job you get, the better was the school you went
to.

That's why Philips-Andover, or Harvard, rank
so highly. Harvard grads start out way up the
ladder in every profession. They are grateful,
and when they grow up, they perpetuate this by
bestowing the best they have to offer on the new
Harvard grads they hire; and by giving big dona-
tions to Harvard. So it goes for Yale, Dartmouth
and all the others.

So what kind of a school is most likely
today, at the end of the twentieth century, to
prepare a student best for a good career?

We don't really have to struggle with the
answer. Everyone is writing about it. This is
the post industrial age. The age of information.
The age of services. The age of imagination,
creativity, and entrepreneurialism. The future
belongs to people who can stretch their minds to
handle, mold, shape, organize, play with new
material, old material, new ideas, old ideas, new
facts, old facts.

These kind of activities don't take place in
the average school even on an extra-curricular
basis. Let alone all day.

At Sudbury Valley, these activities are, in a
sense, the whole curriculum.

Does it sound far-fetched? Perhaps to an
untrained ear. But history and experience are on
our side. How else to explain that fact that all
our graduates, barring none, who wished to go on
to college and graduate school, always got in,
usually to the schools of first choice? With no
transcripts, no records, no reports, no oral or
written school recommendations. What did college
admissions officers see in these students? Why

did they accept them -- often, grab them? Why did
these trained administrators, wallowing in A
averages, glowing letters from teachers, high SAT
scores -- why did they take Sudbury Valley grads?

Of course you know the answer, even if it is
hard to admit; it runs so against the grain.
These trained professionals saw in our students
bright, alert, confident, creative spirits. The
dream of every advanced school.

The record speaks for itself. Our students
are in a huge array of professions (or schools, in
the case of more recent graduates) and vocations.
They are doctors, dancers, musicians, businessmen,
artists, scientists, writers, auto mechanics,
carpenters . . . No need to go on. You can meet
them if you wish.

If a person came to me today and said,
simply: "To what school should I send my child if
I want to be assured that he will get the best
opportunity for career advancement in the field of
his choice?" I would answer without the least
hesitation, "The best in the country for that
purpose is Sudbury Valley." Alas, at present it
is the only one in the country that does the job,
with an eye to the future.

As far as vocations are concerned, Sudbury
Valley has encountered Future Shock head on and
overcome it. No longer is there any need to be
mired in the past.

Moral basics

Now we come to a touchy subject. Schools
should produce good people. That's as broad a
platitude as -- mother and apple pie. Obviously,
we don't want schools to produce bad people.

How to produce good people? There's the rub.
I daresay no one really knows the answer, at least

from what I see around me. But at least we know
something about the subject. We know, and have
(once again) known from ancient times, the absolutely essential ingredient for moral action; the
ingredient without which action is at best amoral,
at worst, immoral.

The ingredient is <u>personal responsibility.</u>

All ethical behavior presupposes it. To be
ethical you must be capable of choosing a path and
accepting full responsibility for the choice, and
for the consequences. You cannot claim to be a
passive instrument of fate, of God, of other men,
of <u>force majeur</u>; such a claim instantly renders
all distinctions between good and evil pointless
and empty. The clay that has been fashioned into
the most beautiful pot in the world can lay no
claim to virtue.

Ethics begins from the proposition that man
is responsible for his acts. This is a given.
Schools cannot change this, or diminish it.
Schools can, however, either acknowledge it or
deny it.

Unfortunately, virtually all schools today
choose in fact to deny that students are personally responsible for their acts, even while the
leaders of these schools pay lip service to the
concept. The denial is threefold: schools do not
permit students to choose their course of action
fully; they do not permit students to embark on
the course, once chosen; and they do not permit
students to suffer the consequences of the course,
once taken. Freedom of choice, freedom of action,
freedom to bear the results of action -- these are
the three great freedoms that constitute personal
responsibility.

It is no news that schools restrict, as a
matter of fundamental policy, the freedoms of
choice and action. But does it surprise you that

schools restrict freedom to bear the consequences
of one's actions? It shouldn't. It has become a
tenet of modern education that the psyche of a
student suffers harm to the extent that it is buf-
feted by the twin evils of adversity and failure.
"Success breeds success" is the password today;
encouragement, letting a person down easy, avoiding disappointing setbacks, the list goes on.

Small wonder that our schools are not noted
for their ethical training. They excuse their
failure by saying that moral education belongs in
the home. To be sure, it does. But does that
exclude it from school?

Back to basics. At Sudbury Valley, the three
freedoms flourish. The buck stops with each person. Responsibility is universal, ever-present,
real. If you have any doubts, come and look at
the school. Watch the students in action. Study
the judicial system. Attend a graduation, where a
student must convince his peers that he is ready
to be responsible for himself in the community at
large, just as he has been at school.

Does Sudbury Valley produce good people? I
think it does. And bad people too. But the good
and the bad have exercised personal responsibility
for their actions at all times, and they realize
that they are fully accountable for their deeds.
That's what sets Sudbury Valley apart.

Social basics

Some time ago it became fashionable to ask
our schools to look after the social acclimatiza-
tion of students. Teach them to get along. Rid
our society of social misfits by nipping the
problem in the bud, at school. Ambitious? Perhaps. But oh, how many people have struggled with
reports from school about their own -- or their

child's -- social adaptations, or lack of them!
Strange, isn't it, how badly people sometimes
screw up what they do? I mean, trying to social-
ize people is hard enough; but the schools seem
almost methodically to have created ways of
defeating this goal.

Take age segregation, for starters. What
genius looked around and got the idea that it was
meaningful to divide people sharply by age? Does
such division take place naturally anywhere? In
industry, do all 21 year old laborers work separately from 20 years olds or 23 year olds? In
business, are there separate rooms for 30 year old
executives and 31 year old executives? Do two
year olds stay apart from one year olds and three
year olds in the playgrounds? Where, where on
earth was this idea conceived? Is anything more
socially damaging than segregating children by
year for fourteen -- often eighteen -- years.

Or take frequent segregation by sex, even in
coed schools, for varieties of activities. Or the
vast chasm between children and adults (have you
ever observed how universal it is for children not
to look adults in the eye?).

And now let's peek into the social situation
created for children within their own age group.
If the schools make it almost impossible for a 12
year old to relate in a normal human fashion to 11
year olds, 13 year olds, adults, etc., what about
other 12 year olds?

No such luck. The primary, almost exclusive
mode of relationship fostered by schools among
children in the same class is -- competition!
Cutthroat competition. The pecking order is the
all-in-all. Who is better than whom, who smarter,
faster, taller, handsomer -- and, of course, who
is worse, stupider, slower, shorter, uglier.

If ever a system was designed effectively to produce competitive, obnoxious, insecure, paranoid, social misfits, the prevailing schools have managed it.

Back to basics.

In the real world, the most important social attribute for a stable, healthy society is co-operation. In the real world, the most important form of competition is against oneself, against goals set for and by a person for his own achievement. In the real world, interpersonal competition for its own sake is widely recognized as pointless and destructive -- yes, even in large corporations and in sports.

In the real world, and in Sudbury Valley, which is a school for the real world.

Political basics

We take it for granted that schools should foster good citizenship. Universal education in this country in particular always kept one eye sharply focused on the goal of making good Americans out of us all.

We all know what America stands for. The guiding principles were clearly laid down by our founding fathers, and steadily elaborated ever since.

This country is a democratic republic. No king, no royalty, no nobility, no inherent hierarchy, no dictator. A government of the people, by the people, for the people. In matters political, majority rule. No taxation without representation.

This country is a nation of laws. No arbitrary authority, no capricious government now giving, now taking. Due process.

This country is a people with rights. Inherent rights. Rights so dear to us that our forefathers refused to ratify the constitution without a Bill of Rights added in writing, immediately.

Knowing all this, we would expect -- nay, insist (one would think) -- that the schools, in training their students to contribute productively to the political stability and growth of America, would --

-- be democratic and non-autocratic;

-- be governed by clear rules and due process;

-- be guardians of individual rights of students.

A student growing up in schools having these features would be ready to move right into society at large.

But the schools, in fact, are distinguished by the total absence of each of the three cardinal American values listed.

They are autocratic -- all of them, even "progressive" schools.

They are lacking in clear guidelines and totally innocent of due process as it applies to alleged disrupters.

They do not recognize the rights of minors.

All except Sudbury Valley, which was founded on these three principles.

I think it is safe to say that the individual liberties so cherished by our ancestors and by each succeeding generation will never be really secure until our youth, throughout the crucial formative years of their minds and spirits, are nurtured in a school environment that embodies these basic American truths.

Back to basics

So you see, Sudbury Valley was started in
1968 by people who thought very hard about
schools, about what schools should be and should
do, about what education is all about in America
today.
We went back to basics. And we stayed
there. And we jealously guarded these basics
against any attempts to compromise them. As we
and our successors shall surely continue to stand
guard.
Intellectual creativity, professional excellence, personal responsibility, social toleration,
political liberty -- all these are the finest
creations of the human spirit. They are delicate
blossoms that require constant care.
All of us who are associated with Sudbury
Valley are proud to contribute to this care.

What Children Don't Learn at SVS

Hanna Greenberg

Sometimes I wonder at our courage. For it does take courage to believe that children who are allowed to spend their school days without the guidance of a prescribed curriculum will in the end be ready to enter the adult world, function in it, and succeed. The truth is that while I have always understood the shortcomings of the prevalent educational system, and felt that SVS would succeed where others failed, I often don't quite know exactly how we achieve our success. Not that this lack of knowledge disturbs me. After all, at the heart of our method is the assumption that one person cannot know what is best for another, so it follows that the children will find their way on their own without our intervention, and often without our comprehending how they did it. Nevertheless, it is sometimes possible to gain insight into the way things work around here, and thus gain more confidence in what we are doing.

Let me give an example.

One of the most striking aspects of the school is the way children play here. Visitors are amazed to see that the school permits the children to play all day, week in week out,

starting in the Fall through the Winter and into
the Spring, year after year. They wonder at the
"country-club atmosphere," or at the "all-day
recess." But that is not what is really striking
about the play at SVS. What is essentially unique
is the utter seriousness, the concentration, even
the passion with which the children pursue their
play. For years I thought nothing of it. I at-
tributed this to human nature, to the fact that
all of us, children and adults, pursue our hobbies
in this manner. It was also obvious to me that
activities which we dislike doing, but which we
must be engaged in out of a sense of duty, most of
us do in a lackluster way, with no enthusiasm,
with minimal output of feeling and imagination,
with a lack of joy and, in general, in a manner
calculated to conserve our energy by avoiding work
as much as possible. We all know this and have
always known this.

One day, however, I noticed some specific
kids whom I have watched play for six years, or
even longer, suddenly (that's how it seemed to me)
latch on to some work with the same dedication
that they applied to their play. This got me to
watch other children, and I discovered this to be
the case with almost all of the people who have
grown up at SVS. They show a remarkable lack of
skill in the art of dodging and shirking. They
seem to have transferred their mode of behavior in
play or fun activities to all their activities.
When questioned, they often admit to lack of interest in certain activities they pursue because
they feel they must, either to learn skills such
as math or spelling, or whatever. In other instances, they take on jobs that are boring when
they need to earn money and no better jobs are
available. Most of the time, they still apply
themselves with energy and concentration to what-

ever they do. They persevere at their work, take
on responsibilities and are esteemed by their
employers. They are also diligent and intelligent
students.

Many learned papers have been written about
the connection between children's games and learning. What strikes me as interesting is how children's play at SVS is related to what they do not
learn here. They do not have to learn to adapt to
activities that they do not initiate. They are
innocent of the techniques that every child uses
sooner or later in the average school throughout
the world. Children who are forced to listen to
teachings that don't answer their quests, who are
forced to study material that does not seem relevant to them, who are grouped together by others
who don't even know them and are forced to learn
together whether they are ready or not, all use
similar methods of coping. I do not have to enu-
merate them; every reader knows some from personal
experience. Slowly the spark of life is diminished, the bright eyes dim, the questions are
left unasked and the life force is wasted on coping with a suffocating environment. Bad work
habits are internalized, character traits are
formed that later require much effort to undo.
When liberation arrives at graduation from high
school it is often too late. Many persons find it
hard to get enthusiastic, to galvanize their
energy for work, to apply their imagination, to be
creative in solving problems.

Children are born with all these qualities
that we all value and reward in adults. Tragi-
cally, our schools educate our young people to
lose them. At SVS we never do teach kids how to
work hard, how to be creative, how to think for
themselves. What we do is not rob them of what
they knew when they were very young. We let them

be, and they do the rest exquisitely all by themselves.

How and What Do Children Learn at SVS?

Daniel Greenberg

No question is raised more often about Sudbury Valley School. Somehow it's easy to accept the fact that the school is a house, or that there are no classrooms. Everybody knows that some of the best progressive schools have moved around the furniture and tried to make things a little less formal, so the fact that there aren't formal study rooms may seem a little peculiar, but it's not that bizarre. What is strange indeed is that nobody seems to be "doing" anything. The school seems to be in perpetual recess.

A little historical perspective can help in grappling with this question. Before we started the school, every discussion of our educational philosophy was a presentation of a hypothetical idea. We would go before a group and say this, that, and the other thing, and people would listen skeptically and present us with one unanswerable objection: "It won't work!" What could we say? That it <u>will</u> work? We were sure that it would work, but we couldn't say it <u>did</u> work.

We know now that it does work. The problem we have now is one not of proving that it will

work, but of trying somehow to explain <u>why</u> it
works when it feels like it shouldn't. That's a
very different problem, a nice kind of problem.

We've had a great many graduates since 1970,
and others who left for one reason or another
without graduating, so we have a lot of experience
with students who have been here and then gone on
to the "outside world." They're in the professions, in the arts, in business; they've gone to
colleges and to trade schools. Everyone who
wanted to go to college got into college. Most
got into the college of their first choice.
People would ask, "How are you going to get them
into college? They have no grades, no recommendations." It's totally against our principles to
write recommendations. The college admissions
applications ask for an evaluation of the students: what percentile of the class are they in,
what their personal characteristics are -- pages
and pages to fill out about the student's character, performance, and abilities and so forth.
Initially people would say, "If you don't fill
that out, how is the student ever going to get
into college?" We've never filled one out in all
the years. We have a form letter which explains
the school and our philosophy and why we don't
fill out the forms. Basically we say, "You people
in the admissions office are going to have to look
at this student and figure out for yourselves
whether he or she is somebody who ought to go to
your school. We're not going to do the work for
you."

As it turned out, what we predicted actually
happened. Admissions people in colleges are
jaded. They get a thousand applications, and
every one of them is the same. There is hardly a
student who has applied to college who isn't "the

best," or who doesn't have twenty letters of
recommendation from twenty different teachers who
say, "Johnny is absolutely the finest student I've
ever had in my 20 years of teaching." What is one
to do? So the admissions people sit there, day in
and day out, looking through all kinds of garbage,
and than all of a sudden somebody applies who has
none of these papers. The applicant says, "I want
to come here. I know I'm the right person for
your school, and I know why I want to be here."
And the admissions people can hardly believe their
ears. Usually, the better the school, the better
the chances are of getting in.

That's just one experience we've had with our
graduates. There are a lot of things we can say
now. For example, we have never had a case of
dyslexia. You read that 10-15% of the population
have dyslexia. But we haven't had one such
instance. It could be an accident. The students
who attended SVS might just happen not to be in
that 10-15%. But it doesn't work that way.
There's no pre-selection of nondyslexic people in
this place. We haven't had dyslexia because we
haven't brought it about.

What we have had is children who have started
reading at a very wide range of ages. We've had
some who started at 4 or 5 (that's what everybody
likes to hear) and we've had others who started at
9, 10, even later. When you look at a person who
isn't reading at the age of 8, you know that person in a standard school setting would be put in a
remedial reading class and subjected to enormous
pressures. But if you stay your course, as we
have stayed our course over the years, and you
leave that person alone and let them develop at
their own pace, the "miracle" always seems to happen. By the time they leave, you wouldn't know

the difference between those who started reading
at four and those who started at eleven.

The point is that today we can relax a little
when we talk about the subject of learning at
SVS. Hundreds of people have been through the
school, and it works -- despite the fact that it's
a "perpetual recess." They go out into the real
world. They make it. They do well. They're
well-adjusted and they're not behind. With that
behind us, we can examine a bit more closely
what's going on and why.

The real problem is that it's hard to tell
what learning is going on, or how it is happening. Learning as a psychological activity is
something truly difficult to get a handle on. We
know very little about the process. There are a
lot of theories, but none of them have stood the
test of time and few are based on hard data or
hypotheses that are supportable. Most educators
know this. In order to cover up for this, in
order to make up for the feeling of inadequacy in
confronting a process that we don't really comprehend, we do what modern man always does. We
label something "learning" and measure it. Then
we're comfortable, because at least then we have
the feeling that we have a grasp on the problem.
We don't really follow the process, but in lieu of
a profound understanding of what's going on, we
find something and say, "Let's declare that to be
learning, by consensus. Then we can measure it
and put it out of our minds." This is basically
what the entire educational system the world over
has done: quantify learning by breaking it up into
measurable pieces -- curricula, courses, hours,
tests, and grades. Take any subject you want: for
example, American history. American history is a
tremendous field. What does it mean to learn

American history? To deal with this, educators
get a book -- Commager, Morrison, whatever, on the
subject. Then they line up thirty people, put
them in a class, and declare, "You're now going to
learn American history. Every day you will read a
certain number of pages of the book, discuss them,
and then take tests on them to make sure you know
what you've read." In this way, they can measure
what is going on. They can say that during the
year, you read 450 pages of American history by an
eminent writer and historian, as a result of which
you "learned" American history. It feels so
comfortable that you never really want to stop to
ask, "Is anybody in this course learning American
history? Does anybody have an overview of the
subject? Has anybody internalized it? Does
anybody remember three years later what they've
supposedly learned?"

The best example of this I ever saw was with
one of the most eminent physicists of our time,
who taught a course in a subject called Statistical Mechanics. He was a Nobel Laureate who certainly knew his subject. He walked into class the
first day, walked up to the blackboard, wrote the
expression "e-H/KT", and started writing a mass of
complex formulas. I went to him after class and
said, "I understand the math and the derivations,
but tell me something. I've read a lot of books
on e-H/KT and I don't understand where it comes
from." He looked at me and said, "I don't want to
deal with that. For me it starts with the mathematical expression 'e-H/KT' and it goes from
there. That's all I want to know about." Even
though he was teaching advanced graduate students,
he was in the perfect tradition of education. He
wanted something he could put his hands on and not
worry about the rest, because the rest was too
subtle and too complex to handle and it didn't

have a place in any organized, quantifiable system.

How did we get to the point where it was so
terribly important for us to quantify learning?
It wasn't always that way. I think it's worth a
thumbnail sketch of the history of education to
understand how we got there.

For most of history there were three quite
distinct forms of education. They had a great
deal to do with social class. There was education
for a small cultural elite, extremely stylized and
formal. People made up their minds what it meant
to be a "cultured person." For example, in 19th-
century Europe, it was cultured to know French,
piano, singing, Latin, Greek, and so on. There
was a universal consensus. Thus it came about
that the entire cultural aristocracy of Russia
spoke French; many didn't even speak Russian. And
everybody learned the piano. It must have been
torture to go to somebody's home for dinner, because no matter where you went, after dinner some-
someone would sit at the piano and give a recital,
and the guests might be expected to join with them
and sing. So, too, with Greek and Latin. Utterly
useless.

One of the best stories about this is told by
Winston Churchill, concerning his own childhood.
He was a total failure in school. To get into his
exclusive high school, he had to go through the
formality of an entrance exam. Of course, he knew
(as did everybody else) that it made no difference, since he'd end up being accepted anyway, as
one of the direct descendants of the Duke of Marl-
borough. But there he was, faced with an entrance
exam in Greek and Latin. He looked at the page
for an hour and finally handed in an empty paper
with his signature on it and a big smudge of ink.
They gave up on him entirely and placed him in the

dummie's class, which learned <u>English</u>! So it happened that Winston Churchill spent his entire high
school career studying English literature, whereas
all the successful "cultured" people learned Greek
and Latin. It hardly needs mention that Churchill
ended up being one of the finest stylists in the
English language in the 20th century.

The moral is very simple. That type of education was a sheer convention. Everybody knew it
for what it was. It was tailored for the elite,
and one conformed to it simply to look right.
That's something that was universal throughout
history, and it all but died at the end of the
19th century, with the death of the elite aristocracy as a class. No matter how much they might
try to keep themselves going, they're gone, and
most of their forms are gone.

The second kind of education that prevailed
throughout history was one that applied to only a
few people: professional training for certain
specific professions. People who were destined to
go into a profession were taken at a young age and
for several years put through a rigorous training
directed solely at the accomplishment of that
profession's aims. An example of this is the
priesthood. In every religion, people who were to
be priests would study the philosophy, theology,
mysteries, the rituals of that religion. It was a
functional education and it was only useful for a
very small number of people at any time.

The great majority of people were subject to
a third educational process, namely learning by
apprenticeship. This meant learning from the
model of accomplished people in the pursuit that
they wanted to follow. The nature of the pursuit
made no difference. If a person wanted to be a
carpenter, he was apprenticed to a carpenter. If
he wanted to be a doctor, he was apprenticed to a

doctor; if a lawyer, he apprenticed to a lawyer;
if a farmer, he worked with a farmer. It wasn't
always a formal apprenticeship, but it always
involved learning by working side by side with
more advanced people. Often, there was a one-on--
one relationship between pupil and teacher.

Good philosophers, good artisans, good musicians, good everything came out of that type of
education throughout history. No doubt the world
could have gone on happily with that method of
education had not a striking shock intervened in
the 18th century which threw everything out of
kilter -- the shock of the Industrial Revolution.

The Industrial Revolution required a mass of
people who were in tune with the machines they
operated. Today many people, especially younger
ones, have no idea what society was like two hundred, or a hundred, years ago. They can't imagine
that it took a day and a half to go from Framingham to Boston. They can't comprehend how Andrew
Jackson could have become the hero of New Orleans
in a battle that he won over the British several
weeks after the peace treaty had been signed in
London ending the War of 1812. It's the same with
the Industrial Revolution. Very few people realize that the kinds of machines that dominated the
18th, 19th, and early 20th century were quite
different from the machines that prevail today.
They were less independent, more limited, and they
needed machine-like people to handle them. That
was the essence of it. They needed people to
perform robot-like, monotonous functions over and
over again and be good at them. This created a
tremendous demand on the society infrastructure
for people to feed this industrial monster.
Everybody went along with this demand because the
end products were something everybody wanted.
They brought material prosperity and made life

better. But they required a tremendous effort on
the part of the people.

Let me try to make this a little clearer.
People who have had experience with developing
countries today know that their biggest problem is
to get the infrastructure in tune with society's
needs. It can't be done overnight. It's a tremendous task. This was brought home to me drama-
tically through an experience in Israel in the
late '50s. I was in Tel Aviv having lunch at a
fancy hotel. All of a sudden, there emerged a
bunch of waiters who looked like they were lost.
Upon inquiry, I found out that they were a group
from an African country who had been sent to
Israel for training in tourist industries. That
country's government had sent twenty or so of
their best high school graduates, and in they
trooped, into the dining room. It was the most
tortuous lunch I ever had, because these people
simply couldn't take an order. They had no idea
how to do it. They weren't at all stupid. They
just weren't "tuned in." All of a sudden I realized that no one stops to think about such things
until they have an experience like this. We can
travel from one end of the United States to the
other, north, south, east and west, and we can
walk into any little drug store, soda fountain,
lunch room, McDonald's, anywhere in this country
-- there are tens of thousands of them -- and
there's basically the same menu on the board
everywhere. We can say, "I want a club sandwich,
or a BLT," and somebody stands behind the counter
and yells, "BLT down!" or whatever, and somebody
in the back makes it, and it comes out and he
writes up a check. Think about it. All over a
country the size of a continent there are tens of
thousands of people for whom this is a totally
natural activity. They weren't born with this.

It didn't come out of the blue. It's almost
unbelievable. It's the product of the infrastructure created by the Industrial Revolution.
It required people who were in a sense interchangeable, just like the machines were. And it
created great mobility. Who ever heard of moving
in the old days? People were born in a place, and
they died in the same place. And their children.
And their grandchildren. Generations on end
stayed in the same town. Today we feel that we're
stable if we don't move for 10 years. You can
take a person from Kansas and stick him in Massachusetts, or from Massachusetts in Oregon -- it's
mind-boggling to understand what this means.
People are interchangeable parts. And the Industrial Revolution is what made them that way.

The educational system responded to the
requirements of the Industrial Revolution in a
carefully thought out manner. 19th Century educators knew what they were doing, and they were very
clear on their aims. They zeroed in on the "3R's"
-- reading, writing, and arithmetic -- as the
basic necessities of the industrial machine. They
needed people who could read instructions, communicate with others in a rudimentary fashion, and
make the elementary calculations required in
everyday work. That's how compulsory education
was born, to fill a specific, narrow need, for a
limited age range of pupils (basically aged 6-12).

Within the limited goals of producing mechanical people for the industrial era, the educational system worked beautifully. Its needs and
its outputs were quantifiable and measurable,
boring and routine. And it had little to do with
the subject of this essay, namely, "learning".

The tensions that arose between the requirements of the Industrial Age and the aspirations of
democracy and freedom were enormous. Nowhere are

they better expressed than in the writings of
Jefferson, whose heart ached as he watched the
industrialization of this country. Jefferson
wished more than anything that America would be
and would remain a rural society, because he was
sure that was the only way we would ever protect
our freedoms. For him, industrialization meant
regimentation and autocracy. This tension between
our political and moral ideals -- to be free, responsible citizens, equal before the law, and equal
with each other -- and the rigid requirements of
an economic system tore the country apart for over
150 years and remains to this day a contradictory
element of our educational system. It is simply
impossible to handle the fact that we treat children fundamentally as prisoners, in the fullest
sense of the term.

I don't mean this to be a polemic, or as an
attack on the schools. It is a plain political
observation. Our concept of a prison and our
concept of a school are analagous; in fact, almost
identical. They involve restraints on the freedom
of movement. They involve physical regimentation. They involve thought control. They involve
obedience and punishment for disobedience. It is
a commonplace that even the architecture of modern
prisons and modern schools has much in common.

The great news is that these tensions don't
have to exist anymore. We're now is the post-
industrial era, an age that has requirements
diametrically opposed to those of the earlier
industrial age. Today the worry is that our educational system is producing human robots. People
are trying to figure out what to do, because
they're not getting graduates out of the schools
who understand how to deal with problems indepen-
dently. What's happened is that the fundamental

nature of the economy has changed. Our machines
are smart enough not to need mechanical people to
run them. That simple fact is the essence of the
post-industrial era. It means that for the
future, what we need is a different educational
product, almost a throwback to the kind of educational product we've had throughout history. We
need people who are selfdriven, self-motivated,
responsible on their own, able to conduct themselves in an intelligent, creative, imaginative
way.

Within this context, I would like to examine
how the basic educational features of SVS fit a
post-industrial democratic civilization. Most
important is the element of freedom. Everyone
knows coercion is counterproductive to learning.
We don't really know what enhances learning; we
don't know the magic button we can press to make a
person learn quickly. But we know the button we
can press to prevent a person from learning effectively: coercion. Most of the people know this
from their own experience, if they face it square-
ly. For example, most adults have hobbies and
interests that are enormously varied, but these
rarely coincide with subject matter that they
learned in school. They spent 12, 16, 20 years,
ostensibly learning all sorts of stuff, but their
real interest lay in constructing harps, sailing
boats, building models, collecting stamps, anything, but hardly ever reading great books! I
remember how shocked I was twenty years ago when
the managing editor of a large publishing company
told me that a very good seller was a book that
sold 10,000 copies -- 10,000 copies to 200,000,000
people! Most people don't read serious books.
They'll read Field and Stream because they're
interested in fishing and hunting, they'll read
just about anything in the areas of their inter-

est, but they never seem to be interested in the
stuff they learned in school.

The second element that's important in this
school has to do with exposure. Children today
are over-exposed. With television, with what they
see and hear around them, they're exposed by the
age of six to things that their parents weren't
exposed to by late adolescence. Exposure per se
is the last thing to worry about. Of more concern
is how to get children away from the relentless
stimulation that is bombarding them on every side.
How are they going to get a chance to sit back and
think -- to contemplate? For us at Sudbury Valley
the best weapon is time. The school is set up in
a way that encourages students to relax, to look
inward to their own internal time and rhythm, to
nurture them. If that requires going through a
period of boredom, that's OK too. Boredom is a
healthy transition between being constantly
assaulted by external stimuli and getting to the
point where you can direct your own internal
life. We have never worried about exposure, and
we have never flinched from boredom, although I
think these are among the hardest things for
parents to handle.

Another key aspect of the school is age-
mixing. The students are not confined to classes
or activities that are prescribed by age groups.
One of the most incredible features of the prevailing school system is how children are segregated by age. Even the so-called open classrooms
only allow a few grades to mix occasionally. It
is a fetish, based on a notion that all people
develop in lock-step, in the same manner, month by
month, year by year -- a theory that runs entirely
contrary to all experience with children young and
old.

Age-mixing is our "secret weapon." It's nothing short of miraculous. The amount of learning and cross-fertilization that takes place defies measurement. You have to see adolescents explaining to six and seven-year olds what the rules of the school are. You have to watch children of all ages teaching each other how to use the photolab, how to use the computer, how to cook, to read, to skate, to play soccer, etc. Age-mixing is the first step towards true apprenticeship.

Another key feature of SVS is its staff, whose primary purpose is to serve the students' needs from a particularly close and vulnerable vantage point. We don't have tenure. And we don't have any inherent power in the school's administration. This is an absolutely central element of the mutual respect that develops between adults and students here. One of the first things that strikes you when walking into SVS is the warmth with which adults are greeted. It may take you aback -- it's almost brashness. It's rarely ever rude. It's equality and openness. All this is an important step towards learning from another person, which can only take place in the absence of fear.

Another key aspect of the school is the judicial system which is designed to give people the feeling, and the reality, of justice for all. The fate of the school is in the hands of the community as a whole, not of a select group of enforcers. It's one of the essential kernels of the democratic process in the school, creating a sense of fairness that has to permeate the school in order for it to work. The minute that people think that things aren't fair, they're going to close themselves off. When they think they're in a fair environment, they can respond openly to each other.

The most important educational concept in the
school is that of responsibility. For each student, as Harry Truman posted on his desk, "the
buck stops here." There is nobody in the school
who will carry the burden for your child and my
child. They each carry it for themselves. It is
impossible to overstate how important this is for
the educational process here.

We saw this vividly when we first opened the
school. In those days, students didn't believe us
when we said to them that they were fully and
solely responsible for their own education. We
told them we would respond to expressed needs, but
we weren't going to direct anyone. Several students thought we didn't really mean it. After
all, we were good guys, progressive educators who,
when the chips were down, were surely going to
come through and bail them out. We had a group of
students who tested us for months. They just
wouldn't get going. They hung around. They
listened to records. But they carefully didn't
"do" anything. They were terribly bored, but they
waited. They were testing us to find out the
answer to a simple question: when would one of us
finally break down and come into that room and put
an arm around one of them and say, "We understand.
We know you're going through hard times. Can we
help you find something interesting things to
do?" That's what they were waiting for, but it
never happened.

One by one they had to break out of their
stagnation on their own. That's the heart of the
whole process. The ability to carry the ball for
yourself.

At the beginning, I said that we don't know
how children learn, at this school or anywhere
else. All we know is that given an environment in

which learning can take place, it happens joyous-
ly, happens excitedly, and happens rapidly.
   I have taught elementary arithmetic at
Sudbury Valley. The first time I taught it I had
a group come to me, between the ages of 9 and 12,
who didn't know any math at all. They were really
hot to trot. So I thought about it a lot. In the
early 60's I had been involved in the development
of the "new math," and I concluded that the new
math is the worst thing that ever happened to
teaching. Before teaching a kid that one plus one
equals two, the new math has to explain the set-
theory background of what this means. What the
kid wants to know is what one plus one is! So I
got a textbook out of our library written in 1898
and went through it with them. We used to meet
for 20 or 25 minutes at a stretch twice a week.
In a grand total of 20 hours of instruction, they
went from not knowing how to add to the end of
sixth grade arithmetic, including fractions, and
percentages, and decimals and the whole bit.
Twenty hours. Because they wanted to learn. I
mentioned this to an experienced educator whose
field was elementary math. He was not in the
least surprised. "We have always known," he said,
"that the math that we teach an hour a day every
day for six years can be learned in a few hours
altogether. We all know that. But the children
hate it, so that there's no way to do it except to
shove it down their throat day in and day out and
hope that over a six year period some of it will
stick."
   How they learn is a mystery. It happens in
different ways for different people. The best we
can do it give a surrounding that will encourage
it to happen. What they learn at SVS is another
story. We don't really care what they learn. We
haven't pre-judged any particular area as being

better to know than another area. Again, in the
early years of the school, we were put to the
test. We would say all fields are equal, but when
we were faced with the reality, we were shaken.
One student wanted to be a mortician. How many
times do you get an adolescent in high school saying he wants to be a mortician? Can you imagine
what a public school advisor would do with that?
"I want to be a scientist" -- yes. But "I want to
be a mortician"?! Now he's become a very successful mortician. At the age of 16 he was doing
autopsies in an apprenticeship program.

Another student that same year told us his
ambition was to be a railroad switchman. That's
all he dreamed about. And he became a railroad
switchman. The point is, when the atmosphere is
free enough that a person can come up to us and
say, "I want to be a railroad switchman," or "I
want to be a mortician," we suddenly realize that
it really is important for us to stick to our
guns; that we're really not going to pre-judge
their interest, because we never can know what the
human mind is going to encompass. What may look
off the beaten track to us may be hailed as a work
of genius five years from now by an admiring
public who cry out, "Look at this daring person
who went off and did something new and exciting!"

What Do Students Choose?

Hanna Greenberg

In the days when Sudbury Valley was a dream about to be realized, I was often asked how we would deal with students who would choose to do only the things that they could do easily, and avoid learning subjects that they would find difficult. In those early days, when theory and not actual experience governed our thinking, I would reply that at SVS we would go along with the students' decision no matter what. We believed that if students were forced to study subjects that they hated or felt inadequate to tackle, then they would probably fail to learn them anyway. We preferred to teach things that were of interest to students rather than coerce them to study material they hated. I do not need to recapitulate here the experiences of educators which attest to the enormous effort it takes to teach an uninterested person material that should be easy to grasp, an effort that in most cases bears no fruit.

That was our situation in 1968. Today we need not theorize in a vacuum. We have experience, and our experience has shown us that our theories were valid although our initial expectations vastly underestimated the results we were to observe. We learned that not coercing students into learning had more far-reaching consequences than we had anticipated. We found over the years that many students not only devote time to learning what they love but choose to learn subjects that they find distasteful or boring. They not only do not choose the path of least resistance, but actually seek out the path that is most difficult for them. This phenomenon is widespread through all age groups, but manifests itself only after the students realize that their destiny is in their own hands and that their direction in life depends on their own actions.

This amazed us years ago when we first understood what was happening; by now, it has become commonplace. Students tell us often that they are studying algebra because they failed to learn it in their previous school. Or they need to do well in the SAT's to improve their chances of getting into the college of their choice, so they study material they find dreadfully boring for months on end. Others force themselves to play outside in order to overcome timidity, physical weakness, or social shyness. Others become active in the administration of the school in order to overcome their inability to organize themselves. The actual activities may vary but the underlying common denominator is conscious and purposeful choice to do what is conceived as most difficult.

Adults love to challenge themselves, and children do so even more. It is human nature to test one's mettle, to seek excitement in exploring the unknown and to enjoy solving problems. The children at SVS have time to do all that and more. They climb their personal Everests every day with courage and vitality. We often are awed by their actions and wonder how such young people possess so much wisdom and foresight to choose the difficult way in order to better their lives.

A New Look at Learning

Daniel Greenberg

I

At the Sudbury Valley School we have encountered a new version of the old story of the parent-child dialogue: "Where did you go?" "Out." "What did you do?" "Nothing." Our version is: "Where do you go?" "Sudbury Valley." "What do you learn?" "Nothing." All too often that seems to be the refrain associated with the school by parents and by people in the community. When the school opened, there was a whole catalogue of objections to what we were doing; as the years have passed most of them have slowly faded away. In the beginning, we were told that the problem was that we were new, and people didn't want to try out a new school before they knew whether it would work or survive, or be accredited. Of course now we're not new anymore, and we have survived, and we have long been accredited. Earlier, there was always the question of how our students could get into college without courses, grades, or transcripts. We had to try to convince people on the basis of abstractions. Now there isn't any question anymore, because any graduate who has wanted to go to college has been admitted. In fact, many of our students have been getting in without our high school diploma. Then

there was the question of how students would be
able to transfer to other schools, in case their
families moved, or they wanted to leave for other
reasons. That too was an objection that people
used as a reason for not enrolling their children
-- because perhaps at some later time they might
have to go to a "regular" school, and then they
wouldn't be able to get back to "reality." Now
that argument has gone, because there are lots of
former students who have gone from SVS to "regular" schools and have done excellently, without
losing time at all. There were so many objections
in the early years! People said the school would
be chaotic; it would be undisciplined; it would be
rowdy; it would be a fiscal nightmare because so
many people have access to money; and on and on.
We used to think that when people finally saw that
the objections were groundless, slowly but surely
they would come around to our way of looking at
things, or at least accept us and think that ours
was a pretty reasonable kind of educational system
for their children and/or themselves. Alas, how
wrong we were! Because there is one fundamental
objection that will probably stay with us for the
forseeable future: namely, that this is a place
where children don't learn anything. It is as
simple as that. People say, "Whatever they do
there -- they may be happy, read, work, whatever
-- one thing is sure: they don't learn anything."
This is something that the students enrolled at
the school hear from their friends, and often from
their parents. They hear it from grand-parents
and aunts and uncles and cousins. We get it from
all kinds of incredulous outsiders who walk into
the school and say that it's very impressive, but
then end with the view that students don't learn
anything here. I think that this is probably the

major factor that keeps new people from enrolling
in droves.

What is really at the heart of the objection? It's not enough to answer by saying, "Yes,
they do learn." We never really know how to
handle it. The proposition seems so ridiculous,
that we often end up saying, in effect, "What do
you mean they don't learn anything? Look at A --
he's learned this. Or look at B. She's learned
this. Or look at this student sitting and reading." We respond with a flood of ad-hoc and
ad-hominem counter-examples, with no real effect.
But such answers don't really relate to the objec-
tors. They look at A reading a book, and that
doesn't satisfy them either. So he's reading a
book! So what? That isn't learning. Nothing
seems to satisfy them.

What, then, is the heart of this objection?
Is it actually true that students don't learn
anything at the school? If not, why do people
think it is true? And what do students learn
here? I'm going to address each of these questions in turn.

In order to get a handle on the whole problem, we have to analyze fairly closely the generally accepted view of learning. In this culture,
the meaning of the word "learning" is closely
determined by four fundamental assumptions. The
first assumption is that one knows what ought to
be learned by people. The second assumption is
that one knows when it ought to be learned. The
third assumption is that one knows how it ought to
be learned. And the fourth assumption is that one
knows by whom each thing ought to be learned.
These four assumptions in essence determine the
meaning of the concept "learning" for this culture. Let's look at them one by one.

II

The first assumption is that we know <u>what</u> ought to be learned. That is to say, the prevailing view is that there is a basic body of knowledge that every human being should know.

It is important to realize that this assumption is not an objective reality. Rather, it is completely determined by the time and the place and the nature of the culture that makes it. In other words, far from being a general truth about knowledge and about learning, it is an assumption that is completely dependent on the state of the culture that makes it. In different eras and in different places, various societies have made -- and still make -- catalogs of what has to be learned. For example, not too long ago, in American culture, there was the simple tenet that the "three R's" were the basics. During the twentieth century, education in this country has been "modernized," and to that list of three R's have been added successively other subjects that were considered equally important. Consider the 19th century in Great Britain: then it was felt that an educated person has to know Greek and Latin literature. In the Middle Ages the "basics" consisted of a course in natural philosophy, speculative philosophy, rhetoric, and so forth, and a very clear avoidance of practical subjects. I don't want to go into a comprehensive history of this subject. I only way to make the simple point that the assumption that we know what ought to be learned is determined completely by the cultural environment, and changes with time. Unfortunately, the one we're stuck with right now in this country was determined by an industrial technological view of our culture that is obsolete.

Indeed, two of the three R's are demonstrably obsolete. Nobody really needs to know arithmetic. Everybody uses pocket calculators, or calculating machines, or computers, or adding machines. No accountant will sit and add long columns of figures by hand, or multiply by long multiplication, or divide by long division. Even the best will make more mistakes by hand than by machine. I can't think of anybody professional who uses arithmetic now. Even people who go out shopping take along their little pocket calculators on which they tote up their expenditures. As far as writing is concerned, that word has many meanings, but certainly two of the main meanings were penmanship and spelling, which were considered very important because people communicated either orally or through writing longhand letters. Today, anybody who's foolish enough to use handwriting is really at a disadvantage in any practical situation. Many schools and colleges don't even accept handwritten papers. Your average letter of application for a job, or your average business correspondence, would never be done longhand. In fact, it's considered an almost esoteric phenomenon if a person drops somebody a handwritten note. And it's equally unimportant to know how to spell. An awful lot of people I know, some of whom are very famous people, don't have the foggiest notion how to spell. One of the things any good secretary is expected to do is to correct all the boss's spelling, and even secretaries don't have to know how to spell: all they have to do is get paid for the time it takes to look up words in the dictionary, or use a word-processing spell-checker.

The point is simply that the concept of curriculum that prevails right through college was determined by the industrial society that this country had in the 19th century. There were certain fundamental skills, methods, procedures, and technologies that were needed in order to keep the industrial machine going. And I don't mean on the blue collar level alone, not only for the people who worked the assembly lines, but also for the secretaries, the accountants, the bookkeepers, and even the executives. The whole industrial machine operated according to some relatively simple robot-like functions that enormous numbers of people had to perform, and for which it was indeed necessary to have a basic, universal common curriculum for everybody. Of course, even then it was a question of whether or not a culture opted to have an industrial economy at all. The large agrarian economies didn't bother with these things. For example, Russia at the time of the revolution was just beginning to decide that it wanted to get into the industrial era, and the illiteracy rate was something like 95%. It just wasn't important for a mass rural culture to know the three R's. In fact, in the entire society there was only a small cadre of people who could write. Everyone else would go to these scribes to have all their letters and documents written or read for them. But for the population at large, it wasn't essential to know how to read or write or calculate or do any such thing in order to till the land or build the houses or do the kinds of activities that were central to an agrarian society.

Times change. In this country, we have come to the point where most routine tasks do not have to be performed by people, even though often they still are. We have the inherent capability to eliminate from the humanly-operated domain the entire body of automatic, robot-like operations that had to be done by enormous numbers of people. Indeed, the revolution that the modern

communications industry has brought about in
society is quite as profound as the revolution
that mechanization achieved a century or two ago,
when it simply did away with the need for vast
numbers of physical laborers to do heavy work.
(That revolution, too, was not universal; and
there are some societies today where heavy mass
labor is still used.) The new information-proces-
sing technology is now doing away with the need
for droves of workers in industrial plants, or
bookkeepers, or purchasers, or secretaries.
Nowadays, once an industry is computerized, most
of the operations are untouched by human hands.
For example, when you place an order for a book
with a major publisher, virtually everything is
handled by computer. And when the inventory
drops, and they need to order a new printing, the
computer tells the presses to do it. You can
imagine how many thousands of clerks have been
replaced. I was in the publishing industry when
this transition took place, and I worked for two
companies, one of which was automated, and the
other still had all its accounting done by bookkeepers standing behind tall desks just like you
see in old movies--standing and writing longhand
all the thousands of entries that had to be made
day by day. Those bookkeepers don't work there
anymore; even that old-fashioned company has
entered the computer era.

     The point is that robot-like individuals are
not needed any longer in large numbers to man the
industrial machine, and this fact has, at a
stroke, rendered obsolete the entire pedagogical
conception of a basic set of things that have to
be known by everybody. Now we are faced with a
completely different educational problem. I'm not
talking about the Sudbury Valley School, or about
our particular philosophy. What I'm saying

applies to anybody planning an educational system
for the modern era in this country. Nowadays,
instead of preparing a list of subjects that are
necessary for everybody to know, all you can do is
draw up an enormous catalogue of different subjects and activities that are available in the
culture, and then proceed from that point. If you
believe in a planned society, you can try to
apportion a certain number of people to each of
these various fields for the good of society as a
whole. That's a political decision, one which
still doesn't mean, of course, that everybody is
going to learn the same thing. It implies a complete lack of freedom of choice on the part of the
students, but at least it's modern, and it doesn't
make the basic mistake of thinking that everybody
ought to be trained in the same way. The other
major political philosophy that is prevalent in
the world today is that of personal freedom. In
that system, it seems to me that you have to end
up saying that each person should be able to
decide for himself what he wants to do. But the
chief point I want to make is that regardless of
political philosophy, the idea that there is a
basic curriculum that everybody ought to know is
gone.
      Let us return now to the original question,
and let me bring it down to specifics. Say we
have a twelve-year old in the school and somebody
asks, "Is he learning anything?" What they mean
is that they know that every twelve-year-old
should be studying social studies, advanced arithmetic, and English grammar. This is the assumption that underlies the question. So if we
answer, "He is not learning social studies. He is
learning photography, or music, or Greek history"
-- indeed, if we answer that he is learning <u>any-
thing else</u> but social studies, English grammar,

and advanced arithmetic, the questioners will not
be satisfied. As far as they are concerned, as
long as the students in this school who are twelve
years old aren't learning what the society today
thinks every twelve-year-old ought to be learning,
they are not learning. And it's only when people
realize that it's a mistake, no matter what your
philosophy of education is, to think in the late
20th century that all twelve-year-olds ought to be
learning a specific set of subjects -- only when
people realize that this just isn't a viable educational view anymore for modern American society,
only then will they be able to say, "Well, I don't
have to insist that they learn social studies,
arithmetic, and English grammar when they are
twelve. I can accept other subjects, other activities, as valid learning for a twelve-year-old."

                          III

        The second underlying assumption is that one
knows when a subject ought to be learned. This
has a more modern origin that the first assumption. It's only been recently that people have
become arrogant enough to think that they understand the human mind well enough to know in detail
how and when it absorbs and handles knowledge. To
be sure, people always knew that little children
don't quite have the ability to handle things as
well as adults, overall. But people saw that
there was such a variety in how children develop
that no one dared become dogmatic. A Mozart might
play the piano at age three, and a John Stewart
Mill might speak a dozen languages when he was
four; one child would do one thing, another child
did something else. It was only when psychology
became "modern" that it got the idea that there is

a specific, universal track that every mind follows in its development, and that all healthy minds proceed at pretty much the same rate along this track. One of the consequences of this view is that it's bad to be learning the "wrong thing" at the "wrong time." For example, if you are expecting somebody by age two to do a particular thing, and you find that he is not, then you conclude that you have an incipient learning disability. I'm not exaggerating when I say age two. It is becoming much more common to extrapolate into earlier years, and engage in what is called "early detection" of alleged learning disabilities and psychological problems.

It is considered a property of the human mind that certain mathematical skills, certain scientific skills, and certain skills of reasoning are acquired at certain ages. As a result, it becomes important (according to this view) that schools provide exactly the "right material" at the right age. Also, it is considered bad to give third grade work to first grade students, because this doesn't develop their minds along the proper track. I think everybody is aware of these views.

One of the things that set me to thinking about this whole subject was a nightmare I had one night. I dreamt that just as we have schools now where all six-year-olds are put through drills in reading, and are drilled and drilled at it, whether or not they are interested in it -- and if they don't achieve at the proper rate, they are immediately tagged and put into a special category and given special teachers -- what I dreamt was that the same thing was happening to one and two-year-olds with regards to speaking. I suddenly saw a school for toddlers where they were all being taught how to speak, just the way we teach how to read, syllable by syllable, word by word.

And if they weren't proceeding at the programmed
pace they were going to be placed immediately into
the "speaking disability category," and so forth.
Perhaps this sounds ridiculous, but after all,
we've totally accepted this attitude when it comes
to reading. Why not speaking? And if you have a
three-year-old who is speaking at a "two-year-old
level," why not put him in the Special Ed. class?
It's a nightmare, and I think it's well on it's
way to happening.
     So again you ask yourself, where does this
come from? How do these psychologists pull it
off? Why was the society in general, and the
professionals in psychology in particular, so
eager to accept this kind of approach? Again, I
think the answer goes back to my old theme. The
so called science of psychology today is the
natural child of the 19th century industrial-
technological-scientific world view, which insis-
ted on reducing everything in the world to a
linear, tracked, simple series of progressions.
This was essentially the definition of knowledge
in any field. There was no such thing as real,
solid knowledge that was not perfectly ordered, in
an exact sequence of rational steps. If it wasn't
ordered in that way it was non-scientific, it was
"art," and as art it was allegedly the product of
the emotions and of the feelings and not of the
mind. Products of the intellect, by contrast, had
to be "scientific." I don't think it's surprising
people reached this view, because they were living
in an era when everybody was drunk with the success of linear technology in the material world.
After all, the view was appropriate to machines,
to mass production, to the assembly line, to
industrialization, to any enormous technological
venture. It was true that those enterprises were
ordered in a precise, linear fashion. So central

was the industrial materialistic view of the
world, that it engulfed all of knowledge, and the
universal aspiration of the intellectual world was
to be included under the umbrella of "science," in
order to be legitimate. Indeed, if anybody came
along and said, "My field doesn't want to be
organized in a logical, rational way," they ran
the risk of being told "If you can't show us the
track of knowledge in your field, you're not
really worthy of being a bona-fide subject." This
approach was a perfectly natural product of the
enthusiasm with technology that gripped Western
society in the 19th century. People were consumed
with a passion to extrapolate the technological
world view to absolutely everything. And the
fields of social theory and psychology were swept
right along with all the others.

If you understand, then, that there is a deep
yearning on the part of social scientists and
psychologists to be "scientific" and along comes a
person who purports to give, on the basis of what
looks to be a very nice scientific work, a good
linear theory of the mind, you can see why they
will jump at it. And it comes then as no surprise
that people like Piaget or Skinner rapidly become
widely accepted by their colleagues, because they
rescued the profession of psychology from the
oblivion of being an "art" and turned it into a
scientific discipline. I think that this idea is
going to fall by the wayside eventually, but it's
only going to happen when the whole culture begins
retracting from the technological world view. You
can see a trend in that direction in modern thinkers today. There are books being published by
very eminent social scientists who are beginning
to say, "This view of human knowledge really isn't
valid. It doesn't take into account the subtleties. It doesn't take into account the complex-

ities. It doesn't take into account innovation.
It doesn't take into account change. It doesn't
take into account the emergence of new theories,
new ideas. It simply isn't adequate to explain
what the human mind has done with the world."
This is being said by more and more people who
have a name in their fields. Whether their voice
is going to prevail in the long run I don't know,
because certainly in the short run the trend is
toward a more feverish technologization of the
social sciences. I think we are going to have a
major struggle on this issue in this country,
although for the time being the forces of technology are probably on top.

                          IV

        The third assumption generally made is that
one knows how any subject ought to be learned,
that there is a "proper" approach, a "correct way"
to study a subject. Even if we have in our school
a person who is learning what "ought" to be
learned -- for example, social studies -- at the
"right" time -- namely, at age twelve -- if the
person isn't learning it in the "right" manner
from the "right" textbook, it's not considered
valid. The extent to which this has taken over
education is astounding. It used to be widely
accepted that there were a tremendous variety of
approaches to any subject. One went to different
schools, even travelled to different countries, to
hear different people develop a specific subject
in different ways. One went to a particular
teacher because he had a fascinating way of presenting a certain subject. This was an accepted
feature of learning. Any subject was thought to
be varied, complex and intricate, and every

original mind was thought to have a different way
of looking at it. It was once considered the
height of absurdity to say that there is a "best"
way to teach physics, or social studies, or
anything. Alas, pedagogy, too, wanted to become a
science, no less than psychology. Pedagogy too
had to become an exact, technological field. The
obvious result was that everything had to be done
in the same way or it wasn't valid. All textbooks
in a given field have to be the same. That's
almost an axiom of publishing today. If you submit
a textbook manuscript to a publisher that deviates
from the accepted way, you'll get a rejection
slip. It may be a great book, but if it is not
the way the subject is taught in schools, they
won't want to publish it. Of course, in a sense
publishers are just representing the prevailing
view. They are marketing agents, and they don't
want to get stuck with a book that won't sell.
What they are saying is that nobody out there in
the educational world is going to use a book that
is any different from the book that is used by
everyone else.

    I don't have to belabor this. It's an exact
consequence of the kind of thinking that I was
talking about earlier with regard to psychology.
And in order to please somebody who is looking at
Sudbury Valley in terms of the prevailing educational atmosphere, our shelves should be filled
with the current editions of textbooks in all
fields that are being studied in other schools.
That would be a "good" library. Our library has a
lot of books in it, and they are very varied, but
it basically cannot be considered a "good" school
library as far as educators are concerned because
in any given subject they are going to look around
here and not going to find only the "right" book

in most fields. And the same applies to any student learning with the aid of any of these books.

I think, again, that in this regard a lot of people who stop to think about it realize that there is a basic flaw in the idea, regardless of their philosophy of education. The flaw is that it rules out completely any concept of innovation in a field. What's missing is any reference to how any one of the subjects being taught in school has ever changed or progressed. The textbooks always deal with static subjects presented "correctly." To me this is an internal inconsistency that should be obvious to anybody. I can only hope that eventually this contradiction will come to somebody's attention in teachers' colleges. Or perhaps this view will disintegrate on its own. As long as you assume that pedagogy is an art, or has variety, you are never under pressure to be right. You only have to have your own approach. You go to hear a teacher, and you either like his approach or you don't like his approach, but you don't ask whether his approach is "right." You say that it is self-consistent, or interesting, but it is not a question of being right or not. But in the present educational system people are constantly plagued with the problem of finding the "right" approach, and each time they find one they label it "right," and it becomes very embarrassing a year or two later to be faced with a situation where it turns out that it wasn't right after all. That leads to a lot of problems. There is always a "new" reading program. Every two or three years there is a whole new "right" way to teach reading, because the last "right" way didn't work. The educational world is constantly being embarrassed, only they don't ever seem to be ashamed of the fact that they were wrong. I guess there is always a hope that between the fact that

they never seem to do the right thing, and the
fact that actually there is no right thing, it may
dawn on people eventually that the whole approach
is invalid from beginning to end.

V

     The fourth assumption is that one knows how
to identify by whom any given subject ought to be
learned. In a way this is the most insidious of
all assumptions, but it follows directly from all
the other points I have made. Our schools have a
sophisticated and ever-improving system for track-
ing people, and for finding out at an ever earlier
age what specific "aptitudes" a person has, so
that a precise, narrow track can be determined for
this person to follow throughout life. In this
society, such a process is exceptionally subtle,
because it involves an authoritarian approach
within a free culture. By employing a variety of
ruses the system produces a process which allows
it to inhibit personal freedom without really
feeling that this is what is going on. The person
doesn't feel that something arbitrary is being
done to him -- which is in fact what is happening. Instead, the system creates the impression
that it is simply looking out for his own best
future, trying to find out what his needs are, and
helping him fulfill them. The fact that others
are deciding what his needs and interests are,
what he is going to do with his life, is covered
over by the illusion that really it is only his
needs that are being considered. Now this is a
combination of all the evils we have talked about.
The assumption is that psychologically one knows
enough about the mind to identify aptitudes; and a
further assumption is that once one knows apti-

tudes, one also knows how to track a person so he will in fact reach the goal that is being set out for him. The whole approach is the ultimate in pedagogical and psychological technology. The only trouble is that it is humanly absurd. All you have to do is read biographies to discover how, time and again, attempts to identify a person's interests at an early age failed. To be sure, sometimes a person of three or four does give very definite indications of where he is heading, but most of the time quite the opposite is the case, and very often people show their true aptitudes only in their 20's and 30's and sometimes much later.

I think that we can understand why people in this society are going to feel, no matter what, that students at Sudbury Valley don't learn anything. They are bound to feel that way. There is just no way out. Because we are not fulfilling any of the four basic assumptions that define the new meaning of "learning" for our culture. And there is no way our philosophy allows us to act on any of these assumptions. So there is no point answering a person, "Look, A is reading a book, and B is learning this and that." Our approach just doesn't fit the whole society's frame of reference, and it's not going to fit until the outside world drops the assumptions that underlie its view of education.

VI

Still, the question remains: Do people learn anything at Sudbury Valley? Obviously to us, the answer is "yes," from our perspective on the word "learning" -- a perspective that may not be

currently popular, but is nevertheless rooted in
our culture's history.

The kinds of learning processes that I see
occurring at the school all the time fall into
four major categories. First, I think we have
learning going on here in the development of personal character traits. Right off, that doesn't
sound like "learning." But actually, character
education has always historically been considered
an important part of education, and even today
gets a lot of lip service paid to it. Unfortunately, in the current educational system, it's
talked about but nobody has any idea what to do
about it. I think that we have developed a setting in which it can be shown that certain character traits are enhanced--traits like independence,
self-reliance, confidence, open-mindedness, toler-
ance of differences, the ability to concentrate,
the ability to focus, and resilience in the face
of adversity. Every one of these traits tends to
thrive in people who stay here for any length of
time. Indeed, the society at large sees the opposite traits being enhanced in their educational
institutions and they worry about it. They worry
about the fact that their settings seem to encourage dependence, a "follower" mentality that
relies on others' judgments rather than on one's
own. They worry about the fact that such a high
percentage of people are insecure, intolerant,
unable to concentrate on their work, and not resi-
lient to failure.

The second major type of learning that goes
on here is in the domain of social etiquette. For
example, children in this school are at ease with
people of all ages and backgrounds and types
(instead of the widespread trait that you see
among children of the same age in public schools
whose tendency is to turn aside, not to look an

adult in the eyes, to be ill at ease, to shuffle, and to mumble). There is the characteristic of being considerate of other people's needs -- a trait that I think is fostered mainly by our judicial system. There is a fundamental acceptance that other people have rights, that other people have needs, that other people have domains of their own that have to be respected. Then there is the trait of being articulate (people are often so inarticulate in the outside world!). And the traits of openness and trust -- I am very reluctant to use those words, but not quite as much as I was in 1968, when they were catchwords for a social fad -- as opposed to the suspicion and paranoia that seem to be rampant in the society, especially among teenagers. And also, there is a certain basic friendliness and courtesy that pervades relationships in the school.

A third category of learning that goes on is in the domain of academic subjects, where we not only see the acquisition of knowledge occurring, but we also find it taking place in ways that other schools would find unusual. For example, people do learn how to read in this school, sooner or later. It's intriguing to watch closely how this happens in each case, because it happens at different ages, and in completely different ways. I don't want to go into any details now, but just by way of example: some learn how to read by being read to over and over and practicing a book until they learn it by heart and start memorizing the words; others learn by piecing together syllables that they have picked up one by one; others learn by trying to associate letters with phonetic sounds. Each one does it in his own way, and at his own initiative.

Substantive learning goes on here in the fundamentals of arithmetic. It goes on in the

principles of democratic government, and in current events. (This is actually rather interesting. The children in this school are generally up
to date on what's going on in the world even
though we don't have "social studies" classes.)
There is substantive learning going on here in the
domestic arts, including money management, taking
care of yourself, survival, cooking, sewing,
childrearing -- a whole group of subjects which in
other schools are relegated to a tertiary place,
for poor learners or for girls, though the subjects are clearly central to living a good life.
Here it goes on in ways that have nothing to do
with age or sex or even with future career inten-
tions. The list of different specific subjects
learned by different people goes on and on --
writing, management, painting, music, etc. -- and
it covers a broad spectrum of conventional and un-
conventional subjects.

Finally, there is a fourth category of learning that goes on here in a way that is not even
remotely matched by any other environment, and
that is the category of methodology. To be sure,
there is a tremendous amount of writing done, for
example, on the techniques of problem solving.
But again, it's assumed in the usual technological
way that there is a "method" for solving problems,
and what one should do in school is teach this
method. The only trouble is, the basic assumption
is again false. If there was a method for solving
problems, we wouldn't have any problems left. The
whole point of a problem is that you don't know
either its solution or the exact right method to
solve it -- if there is one. The idea that there
are multiple approaches to problem solving, that
there are lots of parallel paths that can be ex-
plored, that some are better than others, that
they have to be compared, that there are all kinds

of consequences that have to be followed out in
order to make these comparisons -- the really
complex notions of what problem solving entails
are an everyday feature of this school. Students
have to deal with them every minute of the day in
different areas. From small problems like how to
get hold of a piece of equipment, or what do next,
to major problems like what am I going to do with
my life, or how do I study a certain field, or how
do I answer the questions posed in the book I am
reading, and so forth. Sudbury Valley does it
better than anybody else. Students here also
learn how to use resources, both human and archi-
val. To be sure, in other schools somewhere
around fifth or sixth grade they take the children
to the library and describe the Dewey decimal
system, and the librarian gives a talk on how to
use the library. We all went through this, but
most people never can figure out how to use the
library anyway, and don't. Anybody who has taught
in college or graduate school knows that many
graduate students have difficulty using the
resources at their disposal. It's something that
they have got to learn, and they have also got to
figure out how to find the people who can help
them. At Sudbury Valley we take all this for
granted -- the idea that when you want to learn
something you have got to find someone who is an
expert in it to help you, and you have got to
figure out where you can find the resources in our
library, or in an outside one. These ideas, and
how to implement them, are commonplace around
here.

Perhaps it is fitting to end with something
that Tolstoy wrote about 100 years ago. He wrote:
"Don't be afraid! There will be Latin and rhetoric, and they will exist in another hundred years,
simply because the medicine is bought, so we must

drink it (as a patient said). I doubt whether the
thoughts which I have expressed perhaps indis-
tinctly, awkwardly, inconclusively, will become
generally accepted in another hundred years; it is
not likely that within a hundred years all those
ready-made institutions-schools, gymnasia, and
universities -- will die, and that within that
time there will grow freely formed institutions,
having for their basis the freedom of the learning
generation." Here was a great thinker writing in
the 1860's that it would take another 100 years
for these ideas to come to fruition. A century
later, we were founded. It's uncanny. Will it
take another 100 years to catch on?

The Art of Doing Nothing

Hanna Greenberg

"Where do you work?"
"At Sudbury Valley School."
"What do you do?"
"Nothing."
Doing nothing at Sudbury Valley requires a
great deal of energy and discipline, and many
years of experience. I get better at it every
year, and it amuses me to see how I and others
struggle with the inner conflict that arises in us
inevitably. The conflict is between wanting to do
things for people, to impart your knowledge and to
pass on your hard earned wisdom, and the realiza-
tion that the children have to do their learning
under their own steam and at their own pace.
Their use of us is dictated by their wishes, not
ours. We have to be there when asked, not when we
decide we should be.

Teaching, inspiring, and giving advice are
all natural activities that adults of all cultures
and places seem to engage in around children.
Without these activities, each generation would
have to invent everything anew, from the wheel to
the ten commandments, metal working to farming.
Man passes his knowledge to the young from generation to generation, at home, in the community, at
the workplace -- and supposedly at school. Unfortunately, the more today's schools endeavor to

give individual students guidance, the more they
harm the children. This statement requires
explanation, since it seems to contradict what I
have just said, namely, that adults always help
children learn how to enter the world and become
useful in it. What I have learned, very slowly
and painfully over the years, is that children
make vital decisions for themselves in ways that
no adults could have anticipated or even imagined.

Consider the simple fact that at SVS, many
students have decided to tackle algebra not
because they need to know it, or even find it
interesting, but because it is hard for them, it's
boring, and they are bad at it. They need to
overcome their fear, their feeling of inadequacy,
their lack of discipline. Time and again, students who have made this decision achieve their
stated goal and take a huge step in building their
egos, their confidence, and their character. So
why does this not happen when all children are
required or encouraged to take algebra in high
school? The answer is simple. To overcome a
psychological hurdle one has to be ready to make a
personal commitment. Such a state of mind is
reached only after intense contemplation and self
analysis, and cannot be prescribed by others, nor
can it be created for a group. In every case it
is an individual struggle, and when it succeeds it
is an individual triumph. Teachers can only help
when asked, and their contribution to the process
is slight compared to the work that the student
does.

The case of algebra is easy to grasp but not
quite as revealing as two examples that came to
light at recent thesis defenses. One person to
whom I have been very close, and whom I could
easily have deluded myself into thinking that I
had "guided" truly shocked me when, contrary to my

"wisdom," she found it more useful to use her time
at school to concentrate on socializing and organizing dances than to hone the writing skills that
she would need for her chosen career as a jour-
nalist. It would not have occurred to any of the
adults involved with this particular student's
education to advise or suggest the course of
action that she wisely charted for herself, guided
only by inner knowledge and instinct. She had
problems which first she realized and then she
proceeded to solve in creative and personal ways.
By dealing with people directly rather than observing them from the sidelines, she learned more
about them and consequently achieved greater depth
and insights, which in turn led to improved writing. Would writing exercises in English class
have achieved that better for her? I doubt it.

    Or what about the person who loved to read,
and lost that love after a while at SVS? For a
long time she felt that she had lost her ambition,
her intellect, and her love of learning because
all she did was play outdoors. After many years
she realized that she had buried herself in books
as an escape from facing the outside world. Only
after she was able to overcome her social problems, and only after she learned to enjoy the
outdoors and physical activities, did she return
to her beloved books. Now they are not an escape,
but a window to knowledge and new experience.
Would I or any other teacher have known how to
guide her as wisely as she had guided herself? I
don't think so.

    As I was writing this another example from
many years ago came to mind. It illustrates how
the usual sort of positive encouragement and
enrichment can be counterproductive and highly
limiting. The student in question was obviously
intelligent, diligent and studious. Early on, any

test would have shown he had a marked talent in
mathematics. What he actually did for most of his
ten years at SVS was play sports, read literature,
and later in his teens, play classical music on
the piano. He studied algebra mostly on his own
but seemed to have devoted only a little of his
time to mathematics. Now, at the age of twenty-
four, he is a graduate student in abstract mathematics and doing extremely well at one of the
finest universities. I shudder to think what
would have happened to him had we "helped" him
during his years here to accumulate more knowledge
of math, at the expense of the activities he chose
to prefer. Would he have had the inner strength,
as a little boy, to withstand our praise and flat-
tery and stick to his guns and read books, fool
around with sports, and play music? Or would he
have opted for being an "excellent student" in
math and science and grown up with his quest for
knowledge in other fields unfulfilled? Or would
he have tried to do it all? And at what cost?

As a counterpoint to the previous example I
would like to cite another case which illustrates
yet another aspect of our approach. A few years
ago a teenage girl who had been a student at SVS
since she was five told me quite angrily that she
had wasted two years and learned nothing. I did
not agree with her assessment of herself, but I
did not feel like arguing with her, so I just
said, "If you learned how bad it is to waste time,
why then you could not have learned a better
lesson so early in life, a lesson that will be of
value for the rest of your days." That reply
calmed her, and I believe it is a good illustra-
tion of the value of allowing young people to make
mistakes and learn from them, rather than direct-
ing their lives in an effort to avoid mistakes.

Why not let each person make their own decisions about their use of their own time? This
would increase the likelihood of people growing up
fulfilling their own unique educational needs
without being confused by us adults who could
never know enough or be wise enough to advise them
properly.

So I am teaching myself to do nothing, and
the more I am able to do it, the better is my
work. Please don't draw the conclusion that the
staff is superfluous. You might say to yourself
that the children almost run the school themselves, so why have so many staff, just to sit
around and do nothing. The truth is that the
school and the students need us. We are there to
watch and nurture the school as an institution and
the students and individuals.

The process of self direction, or blazing
your own way, indeed of living your life rather
than passing your time, is natural but not self
evident to children growing up in our civilization. To reach that state of mind they need an
environment that is like a family, on a larger
scale than the nuclear family, but nonetheless
supportive and safe. The staff, by being atten-
tive and caring and at the same time not directive
and coercive, gives the children the courage and
the impetus to listen to their own inner selves.
They know that we are competent as any adult to
guide them, but our refusal to do so is a pedagogical tool actively used to teach them to listen
only to themselves and not to others who, at best,
know only half the facts about them.

Our abstaining from telling students what to
do is not perceived by them as a lack of something, an emptiness. Rather it is the impetus for
them to forge their own way not under our guidance
but under our caring and supportive concern. For

it takes work and courage to do what they do for
and by themselves. It cannot be done in a vacuum
of isolation, but thrives in a vital and complex
community which the staff stabilizes and per-
petuates.

Wrong Questions, Wrong Answers

Daniel Greenberg

Everyone has heard the aphorism, "To get the right answers, you have to ask the right questions." Much energy has been expended on trying to discover how to formulate "right questions" in any field of endeavor. But people seldom give much thought to the obverse dictum. At Sudbury Valley, it has more significance than the original.

No matter how much people read or hear about the school, no matter how many thesis defenses they attend, no matter how many graduates they encounter, they inevitably come around to the same old query: "What courses do you have?" In an era characterized by the quest for simple, unambiguous solutions, "courses" are thought to cure ignorance much as penicillin cures bacterial disease. They are the magic bullet, the universal panacea. In high school, a certain specified number of courses means a diploma. In college, the right mixture produces a degree. In the professions, course credits mean financial and career advancement. In business, they mark the road toward the Executive Suites. Do you want your car repaired properly? The TV ad tells you to go to the dealer whose

servicemen have course certificates on the wall.
Courses are the rites of passage, everywhere. It
hardly makes a difference what the contents are,
or whether they are retained for any length of
time. (When I was teaching Physics at the university level, I remember sitting around with colleagues on the faculty who would laughingly admit
that they couldn't come close to passing the
courses that were being taught to their students.)

To ask students at Sudbury Valley what
courses they are taking is to ask the wrong question. No conceivable reply can be proper. If the
students being queried change the subject, they
are being evasive. If they say "none," they are
being outrageous (or hopelessly anti-intellec-
tual). If they rattle off a list, they are saying
nothing meaningful, and they know it.

What is, after all, a "course"? The very
name is the answer to the question. It is a
designated path for the flow of a selected collection of information. The instructor, the person
who determines the course, picks the material, the
method of presentation, the connections, and the
rate of progress. The instructor's path is not
the only path, nor is there any reason to believe
that it is the best of the infinite number of
paths available. The "best" cannot even be said
to exist at all. More important, there is no
possible way that any two people's paths for
organizing a subject could possibly be the same.
No two minds work the same way.

A course, then, is a glimpse into the
instructor's way of organizing, and thinking
about, a subject. As such, it is a curio. For
the most part, for the overwhelming majority of
instances, it is of no more lasting value to the
listeners than a glimpse of a passing scene. At
best, in some rare and lucky instances, it serves

as a spark to provide insight, to trigger another
person's own private train of thought. When
courses are given to willing participants, it is a
form of entertainment -- like a movie, a play, a
reading, a concert, a show. When courses are
given to unwilling participants, it leaves behind
scars of hostility, anger, and apathy.

Sudbury Valley School was established not as
yet another institution to enshrine courses, but
as its antithesis, a place where the internal
growth and personal path of each student is sacro-
sanct. The processes that have value at Sudbury
Valley are the private ones that take place within
the minds and souls of each student. To find out
the real value of Sudbury Valley, one has to ask
personal questions; and to do that, one has to
first take the trouble to forge a relationship
that enables such questions to be answered.
Parents who have close personal bonds with their
children, peers who are friends, teachers who have
shown real caring, these people can ask, at our
school, "What is going on with you these days?"
They will be graced with real answers -- not with
course lists, or with silence, or with anger, but
with the flow of internal revelation that constitutes truth.

Ask the wrong questions -- get the wrong
answers.

Do People Learn from Courses?

Daniel Greenberg

There is continuing pressure on the part of
the outside educational community to make people
at the school feel that there is something defec-
tive in a person's education if he hasn't had
certain formal courses in certain subjects. This
pressure plays on the insecurity of many students
who wonder, "Can I really go into a certain field
if I haven't had courses in it, if I haven't had
formal schooling in it and learned it 'properly'?" An uneasy feeling is generated that a
person just can't do something right if he doesn't
have an "adequate" course background in it. In
fact, it is virtually universal that if you go to
somebody and say, "I want to become an X, or Y, or
Z," the first kind of advice you get is to take
courses and get a formal degree in the subject,
because that way you will get the knowledge you
need to do the work, whether it is laboratory work
or history or English literature or anything else.
So I want to address myself to this question,
because a lot of times we are asked, "Do you have
courses?". It is not so much that I want to discuss whether or not we have courses, but I would
like to focus on the more basic question of how
one learns something, and in particular what
relationship does taking a course have to how one
learns things.

As I see it, there are three levels of
learning that take place in every person. The
first I would like to call "curious probing." It
consists of superficial attacks on the environment, or on any particular subject. It is something random, something accidental; it has to do
with a person reaching out to grapple with things
that happen to him or he comes across in his
environment. It is rapid, it is triggered by
something that happens; it is not the result of
contemplation. You come across something and you
want to know more about it, so you ask a question,
or you are curious about it and you go to the library and get a book about it and think about it
for a while. Most of this curious probing never
leads anywhere serious. It is filed away, it just
becomes part of the great reservoir of the subcon-
scious that you may call upon later to make some
interesting associations when you do some really
important work. It has no direct followup.

I think it is important to understand that
the very nature of curious probing is superficial. That's a desirable characteristic in this
case. The fact that you don't follow up isn't a
defect in this kind of learning; on the contrary,
it is the essence of this kind of learning, because it is meant to be scattershot, it is meant
to introduce you to as many different things and
stimuli as possible. Our formal educational
system has emasculated curious probing terribly,
because it has made of virtue of "follow-up", and
thus has robbed the probing of its most essential
aspects, namely, spontaneity and rapidity. If you
want a vivid picture of what I am talking about,
look at any "progressive" school. These schools
pride themselves in being very sensitive to the
interests of children; they boast that they pick
up all the leads provided by the children and try

to follow them out. A really good progressive
school teacher is one who watches a child closely,
who observes that first glimmer of interest in,
say, a rock, and who then promptly comes forward
and tells the child, "Oh, you are interested in
rocks; we have a wonderful collection of books on
geology, etc." This approach is a turn-off to
curiosity. What the child learns in an environment like that is that it doesn't pay to probe,
and if you do, you have got to hide it like a
criminal activity, because if anybody ever catches
you, they will follow up on you and they will get
you involved to a degree that you just don't want
to be and don't feel you ought to be.

Personally, I think that schools respond this
way to initial curiosity as part of a calculated
campaign by the educational establishment to kill
curiosity. You see, there are two ways to kill
curiosity--an efficient way and an inefficient
way. The inefficient way used to be just to
forbid people to do things. This was inefficient
because, while the teacher was standing up lectur-
ing and trying to keep discipline, somebody had
another book hidden under his school book or his
desk, and was curiously probing away. So modern
man found a better way to kill curiosity: simply
to nurture it to death by the follow-up approach,
to grab it, to "love" it, to convert it to something that it isn't and to make a person feel
guilty if he doesn't follow up his first tentative
probes. I think that the modern day student who
is in a "progressive" environment has his curiosity knocked out of him quickly. He learns that
whenever he looks at any kind of interesting thing
he is going to be pounced on. As a result, probing curiosity loses its whole function as a
learning mechanism.

Now we turn to a second level of learning.
When I call it "second" I don't mean to imply that
it is in any sense "between" the first and third.
It is a different kind of learning, and happens to
be number two on my list. This kind of learning I
call "entertainment-style." The primary aim of
the entertainment is having a good time. That's a
perfectly legitimate primary aim: we all like to
go out and have a good time. The second kind of
learning is one that comes as a by-product of
having a good time. Everybody knows that if you
go to Coney Island you learn a lot; there are all
sorts of things going on, it is a fantastic experience. Or consider a movie: you see a movie,
and you may learn a moral message, or you may
learn some little trivia about camera technique or
something else. We know that all kinds of learning can be picked up as a by-product while you are
having a good time. This is painless learning,
and it is in a category of its own because it is
not to be confused with learning as a primary
goal. I'm all for people having a good time, but
if the primary emphasis is on the entertainment
and only the second by-product is learning, then
clearly, almost by definition, this is not an
efficient mechanism for conquering an area of
knowledge. You can get lots of secondary fall-
out, but learning is not the primary goal. On the
other hand, it is a pleasant thing to be entertained. People like to be entertained, people
seek it. And it has been a fact throughout history that people involved in the entertainment
profession have always sought to teach something
on the side. For example, political movements
always seized on the entertainment media as a way
to introduce their program, via ideological
literature, ideological theatre and poetry and
music and so forth. The idea is to seize people's

desire at all ages to have a certain amount of
fun, and to utilize that for other purposes as
well.

The third category of learning that I'd like
to distinguish is learning for the sake of mastering something, for the sake of getting hold of a
field or an area or a subject. This kind of
learning is the opposite of curious probing. For
some reason, a person decides that he is focussed;
the scanning camera has stopped, and it has focussed on a certain scene, and he really wants to get
a clear picture of it. There are many characteristics of this third kind of learning that are
worth noting. Characteristic number one is that
it is unstoppable. It is something that wells up
within a person and becomes a preoccupation.
Indeed, that is what it means to "zero in" on
something. That becomes the only thing you want
to do, it is what you are obsessed with, what you
are totally devoted to and involved with. It is
an incredibly difficult thing to place effective
roadblocks in the path of a person who has really
focussed on something and wants to do it. You
can't discourage them with any of the ordinary
arguments, such as "It's too hard for you, it's
too expensive, it will take you too long, it's too
this or too that." None of these things will work
because the person shows an exceptional degree of
obstinacy and sheer orneriness in pursing what he
wants. This is something that happens all the
time in the Sudbury Valley School. When we first
started the school, we used to have long discussions on how we could tell when a student is
really interested in something. We finally realized that it is really no problem at all. If a
person is really interested in something, they
can't be stopped. So if you really want to find
out, try and stop them. Of course, usually you

don't have any need to find out, so you just let
them go for a while and their interest becomes
evident anyway. You can see it in a whole range
of activities that have happened at school. Any
biography of a person whose achievements we respect will usually stress this point, that the
person got an idea, clung to it, and nothing could
stop him. Biography after biography is just such
a story of how people overcame obstacle after
obstacle to achieve their goals. The hallmark of
learning for the sake of mastering is the enormously potent drive that yields to nothing at
all. Even normal, everyday life drives play second fiddle. You don't eat well for days on end,
you don't sleep enough, you don't think of entertainment, you don't think of sex, you just think
about the thing you want to do and you are totally
taken up with finishing it.

Now from these observations there follows a
second important characteristic: there is no
turning this drive to learn on and off. Time
plays a very important role, in the sense that you
can't be relaxed about it. You can't be told,
"Well, it is very nice that you are interested in
this, but if you come in every morning at nine
o'clock I'll give you fifteen minutes, or an
hour." This is just out of the question. The
person wants to know now. They are ready to sit
down and talk twenty hours in a row, and maybe
that would satisfy them, but stringing it out for
months and months is out of the question. They
want to go to the library now, to read every book
on the shelf.

A third point about learning for mastery is
that it brings with it its own evaluation. It is
an inherently self-evaluative kind of learning, in
the following sense. When you set a goal to con-
quer a certain area you will stop only when you

have convinced yourself that you have achieved
your goal. No one else can convince you that you
have achieved it if you haven't, and if you think
you have, no one else can convince you that you
haven't. How many times have you seen someone
come over to a child and say, "It's all right, you
don't have to go any further, go to sleep now," or
"It's time to turn to something else, it's no good
for you to do nothing but this, you've done enough
in this direction, you're good enough at it." And
the person will insist on going further until
convinced inside that the quest is finished.

When I talk about self-evaluation I mean that
people set their own goals, and determine for
themselves whether they are really satisfied. In
the course of their activity, they will almost
always turn to other people for verification and
for instruction. They will ask how you do this,
how you master this or that skill, does this look
right, does that? They will ask for a lot of
input, opinions and data from other people. But
the ultimate decisions as to whether or not they
are satisfied is theirs and theirs alone. Again,
we know this to be true in situations that have
made history. Think of all the people who have
come up with new theories. We know very well that
the reactions are always negative whenever a
person comes up with anything new. The standard
reaction of the whole world is that this is not
good, it's wrong, it's new, it is different from
what we have always done and from what is right.
Innovators use these reactions to sharpen their
arguments, but they are never a substitute for
theirs own personal determination that what they
are doing feels right.

Having distinguished three types of learning,
we can now return to the question posed in the

title: Do people learn from courses? Reviewing
the three basic categories of learning outlined
above, we can answer the question rather quickly.
Courses cannot play a significant role in a
person's quest to master a field. The very word
"course" tells you what the essence of a course
is. A course is something spread out in orderly
fashion, block by block over a period of time; it
runs along a set path. A course inherently con-
tradicts the immediacy of a drive toward mastery.
And it just won't do because by nature it derives
from external opinion, external evaluation and
external authority.

Now, everyone accepts this viewpoint for
people over the age of 25; this is just another
example of how our culture treats different ages
in different ways. Consider the following proposition. If a mature adult -- say, an academician
-- comes along and says, "I want to switch fields.
I have decided that I'm not going to continue
working in physics, I'm going into history," will
their colleagues think they are going to enroll in
History I and then take a year of History II then
a year of History III, maybe get a B.A. in
History, and then maybe a year later an M.A.? Of
course they are not thinking that. They are
thinking, "Old professor so and so is going into
history -- that means they are going to learn the
field of History." How it is done in detail will
not concern them, but one thing nobody will assume
is that courses will be involved, because it is
absurd. You don't think a mature professor is
going to get anything out of a course. The
professor is obviously going to attack the
material directly.

The role of courses in curious probing has
already been discussed, and there is really nothing to add. Courses simply have no relationship

to curious probing. We are thus left with the role of courses in entertainment learning, where I think they have an important function. Courses are the learning analogs of the soap opera, or magazine serial, or anything like that. They are a stretched out form of entertainment. After all, in our schools we've got to keep the students entertained for eight to ten months, so naturally the solution is similar to the one the television networks adopt. They have to keep the viewers entertained, all day long, month in and month out, and they would get nowhere if they gave a complete show every day; instead, they string out the story over weeks and months. In the same way, schools devise a stretched out entertainment mechanism to keep their clients happy. The entire science of pedagogy from A to Z, on the elementary and secondary and college level, is the science of entertaining students with a hoped-for educational by-product. A course is a way to ensure that your entertainment will continue over a period of time.

I wish to stress that I do not look down on entertainment as a value in itself. But it is absurd for people to confuse the entertainment with learning for mastery. That's where the problems begin. For example, I don't think there has ever been anybody in the Sudbury Valley School who opposed courses, recognizing them for what they are, any more than anyone opposed showing movies or anything like that. But we have never made the mistake of confusing these two functions.

I want to add a word on a related point. There is one kind of lecture course that stands in marked contrast to all the other kinds. Also, it's relatively rare. I am referring to a course that serves a primary function for the lecturer rather than for the hearers. There are times when people come up with new ideas, and as part of developing a way to communicate with the rest of the world, they may give a series of lectures or a course, or engage in some other such interaction with other parties. In that case, the course serves as the first communication of an original work to the world. This serves a crucial role for the creator. It helps clarify ideas, it provides feedback, etc. The only question is, what good is it to the listener? And that's really a puzzling question. If the listener happens to be zeroed in on the subject matter, which is very rare--then an almost miraculous thing takes place; here is the lucky listener, interested in a given subject, and all of a sudden there just happens to be in the vicinity a person who has just created some new thinking on the subject. It is an exhilarating experience, but unfortunately very rare. On the other hand, for most of the hearers such lectures are just a very exceptional form of entertainment -- exceptional because in addition to the usual entertainment value there is the thrill of being among the first to hear the ideas being expressed. I remember many such occasions in physics in the 50's and early 60's. A person would come up with a new theory, and when the first lectures were given, the hall would be electric. The hearers would respond to the burst of creativity, though they couldn't care less about the subject matter per se.

    A school like ours has a place for that kind of lecture course not because it is directly important to the students for the subject matter -- that is a rare accident -- but because it is important to maintaining a vibrant intellectual atmosphere in the school. It should be widely known that we always welcome people who are willing to share with us the first fruits of their creative thoughts.

A Moment of Insight

Hanna Greenberg

One of the most embarrassing questions I am
asked by people who listen to my spiel about how
children learn most of what they need to know on
their own is this: "Let's assume that what you say
is true; then why should they go to SVS at all?
What do you as staff do there for them?"

What am I supposed to say? That I am there
to answer the phone, drive to zoos, to museums, to
hardware stores, to fishing holes and such, and
sometimes to teach them some math or answer
questions about spelling, zoology, or whatever?

The truth is that as staff we do many things,
and one likes to feel that after all these years
we need not worry that students and parents don't
realize what they are. However, since some students who spend years at SVS and never attend
regular classes seem to get as much out of their
school years as those who do have classes, I have
often wondered to myself about the actual teaching
that the staff does. How and when and why do some
children use us as teachers, while others don't
seem to need or want us in that role?

During a recent vacation I got a little
insight to this question. This is how.

Joan Rubin and I have been cross country
skiing for about fifteen years. We had both heard
from Marge Wilson and others what fun it is, so we

bought the skis, poles and boots and when the snow
fell, out we trudged. We had great fun but we
were awful skiers. We never seemed to learn how
to go up or down hill. The snow had to be just
perfect for us. Not too fluffy or too icy. We
kept going out five to ten times a year but we
never made real progress. Then during the vacation we went out one lovely day and proceeded to
fall and slip and slide on the rather icy snow.
On the spur of the moment, we decided to take a
lesson from an experienced teacher. After a mere
two hours we learned so much that hills that had
terrified us became our favorites, and places that
we had tried to avoid at all costs became our
playgrounds. Needless to say we were both elated.

As I was mulling over this experience, it
occurred to me that here were some answers to the
questions I raised about teaching and learning at
SVS. True, many people can figure out how to ski
(or do algebra or read) all by themselves -- but I
didn't. True also that many people learn well
from teachers, as I did with skiing. It seems to
me that people truly interested in a certain subject or activity will work at it until they master
it, whether or not they are aided by others. However, there are some things that people like or
need to know without a major commitment of effort.
In such cases, they can benefit from an expert
because they are unwilling to put in the time
required to figure out the problem on their own.
So it seems that those students who are crazy
about algebra will sit with a book and study it on
their own. Others who want to learn it as a challenge, or to pass the SAT's, are apt to ask us to
teach them. Both categories of students should
have the choice of how to pursue their learning,
alone or with a teacher. Often students will
study some subjects on their own and seek a

teacher for other subjects. I am glad that they can do both at SVS, and thus in each instance find the best way to satisfy their own learning needs.

When Does a Person Make Good Use of His Time?

Daniel Greenberg

I have become more convinced with each passing year that even though a host of problems are raised in connection with the Sudbury Valley School educationally, the root problem people have with the school is whether the people here are going to make good use of their time. That is what really bugs people, whether they are parents, or visitors, or educational critics, or even potential enrollees. "Suppose I send my kid and he spends a year or so at the school. What's he going to do with himself? Is he going to waste his time there?" As a result, we find it necessary to get into philosophical discussions on what's a waste and what's a good use of time.

Even though a lot of other doubts are voiced with respect to the school that have to do more specifically with learning theory, I don't think learning is the primary problem. By now people look around and see that students who have been here for several years are full of life and bright-eyed; that eventually they all teach themselves how to read one way or another; that all those who want to are able to get into college; that they learn enough math to use if they

need it; and so forth. But even when people concede that the learning will be all right and the
career advancement will not be hindered, still
there is something that really bugs them, and
that's the use of time: are students going to
make good use of their time while they are going
to school?

There are all kinds of peculiar fears lurking
behind that worry. Many a parent feels that even
if his child learns everything the parents want
him to learn, and does everything the parents want
him to do, somehow if he hasn't "used his time
well," it's been a waste of money.

Often, we say in reply that one has got to
respect and trust people and that however they use
their time is their own business. That answer is
right, but it only goes part of the way. It
doesn't really address the worry. It's sort of a
moral or political answer: "What I do with my time
is my business, and it is an invasion of my privacy for you to ask about it." That doesn't
answer the real concern of the parent who may even
be ready to concede the political question but
still is worried: "O.K., so I have faith in my
kid, and I'm not going to intervene in his life,
but is he going to do well?" So I think the time
has come to grapple with the question directly.

The answer isn't simple. In fact, there are
so many versions of answers that you know you are
in trouble before you even start. You have people
who say you should never worry about time, time is
just a terrible imposition; you shouldn't be
uptight about it, you should give a person all the
time in the world. These people have a perfectly
relaxed attitude towards time. The trouble is
that these people run into one major roadblock: if
you have ever gone to a country where the entire
population has that attitude toward time, you go

crazy. It is all very nice to say, "Let X use his time any way he wishes," until you visit the Carribean, for example, where the entire cultural milieu has that framework. Everybody feels that there is no rush about anything. And most Americans go crazy after a while. It's nice for a vacation, but nothing that you really want to get done gets done. If you want to build yourself the simplest house, or get yourself outfitted, or make use of something, you find the supplier is asleep or the ship hasn't come in, or someone essential went off to another island, and soon you get to realize that precious little ever gets accomplished. What you expect to take a month or two could take a year or two or never happens at all. Time begins to loom very large in your mind after exposure to this kind of general atmosphere. So the simple, relaxed answer which so many people want to give is really not satisfactory at all.

On the other hand, the neurotic answer that we are exposed to in this culture is just as clearly not the answer. "You've always got to be doing something useful. You have to account for every minute of the day in a productive way. If, when you go to sleep at night, you can't really say that you have used every minute of your time productively, then a piece of your life has flitted by, never to return again. You've just squandered it." That approach may be effective in producing all kinds of results, but the trouble with it is that it calls forth a host of counterexamples of all the great things that we admire in our culture being the result of a relaxed attitude. The frenzied approach never created anything worthwhile. Great physicists, for example, spend oodles of time climbing mountains or sailing on yachts to get their ideas, etc.

In seeking some kind of a comprehensive picture that makes sense, I've come to the conclusion
that the basic need is to understand the unique
amalgamation that makes up Western Culture. It is
only against that background that any use of time
makes sense. What is unique about Western Culture
is its subtle and artful combination of technology
and creativity. By technology I mean all the
aspects of the culture that are methodical, rou-
tinized, go according to fixed rules. These are
the backbone of such activities as engineering.
The technological aspect of the culture is the
part that is rigorously determined within a strict
logical framework.

Every culture has a technological side to
it. That is an inherent part of controlling the
environment: you discover certain fixed relationships which enable you to control your environment. No matter where you live, whether in the
most undeveloped part of the world or in the most
advanced, in order to give your life some order
you always manage to come up with some fixed relationships that serve as guideposts. In our culture, this trend came to be very highly developed
in ancient Greece. There is an historical record
of every step of the development. The Greeks
seized on this aspect of the culture, elevated it,
and made a great art of it. In particular, they
developed the science of logic to an extremely
advanced state. Later, the Romans did the same
with engineering.

The key point about technology is the logic-
ally rigorous aspect of it. You build a bridge on
the basis of relationships that you know are going
to be valid. If it collapses, you don't throw up
your hands and say, "Oh, well, it's some act of
God." Instead, you make an investigation to see
if someone has altered the cement, because you

know that there is cause and effect operating in
bridge-building, and that if it had been done
right the bridge would have stood. The technological aspect of society is hard and fast, linear
and unique; you are dealing with a routine, a
prescription, a known way of doing things. This
is the basis for all of our industrial technology. The technological side of the culture can
-- with a considerable effort, to be sure -- be
reduced to sets of routine operations that are
very carefully defined; to the extent that this
can be done, we can eventually reduce the entire
technology to a completely automated, mechanized
procedure.

During the last two hundred years people got
ever more enmeshed in the technology, especially
in mass production industry. The recent development of computers means that gradually people are
going to be moved out of the technological side a
machines take it over. Now my point here, in
talking about time, is that the greatness of
Western Culture is heavily dependent on technology. Even those who talk about a "return to
nature" depend heavily on the technology to keep
their dreams going.

Let's look at the other strand in the culture
briefly. Creativity is an inherent human trait
and is obviously going to be found in every culture. But again, I think in Western Culture it
has been given tremendous outlets it doesn't have
in other cultures. Consider how we use the media.
In the old days, or in other forms of society, if
a man wrote great poetry maybe only his neighbors
would hear it, or maybe somebody would reduce it
to writing and it would be circulated among a
small number of readers. In our culture, it is
not just that we have printing, it is that we have
an <u>attitude</u> toward it, we <u>want</u> to distribute

literary creations, we want them widely known.
There is a positive attitude towards the distribution of the fruits of creativity in this culture.
It is not enough to say that the printing press
made it possible for people to read great poetry,
or the phonograph made everybody have access to
great music. To be sure, the printing press made
it possible, but it was a positive attitude in the
culture that made it happen, because a printing
press could print nothing but nonsense and phono-
graphs could play nothing but junk. The culture
itself has placed a high premium on its creative
people. It has done everything to make heroes out
of them and distribute the products of their creativity. Somehow Western Culture has had the inner
security to encourage diversity and innovations
more than any other culture. After an initial
burst of creativity, most other cultures settle
into a form that is fairly stultified after a few
centuries. It is a unique feature with us that we
continue to place a premium on creativity, we
continue to welcome innovation generation after
generation, after thousands of years: we live on
change.

That's enough background to deal with the
problem of time. A "good use" of time is relative
to what you're using it for. It depends on which
of the two strands of our culture you are focus-
sing on to answer the question. A person who is
involved in some way in the technological aspect
of the culture is making good use of his time when
he tailors his time carefully and rigorously to
the technological needs which are being called
for. This is the basis for our whole attitude
towards efficiency, towards deadlines, towards
getting things done. If you are going to get into
the technological side, you've got to make a

technological use of time. That's where we part
company with the Carribean Islanders. Because
even when they deal with technology they take it
easy. Even when they build a road, they do not
watch the clock. Now, if you are going to build a
road, if you are going to have to lay down a mile
a week, everybody is going to have to do a certain
amount of work in a certain amount of time; it is
a technological demand that is being made. One
isn't saying, "Let's sit down and create new ideas
about transportation." One is saying, "Let's
build a piece of asphalt road one mile long"; and
there are specified ways of doing it. It's not an
unknown, it's not a contest for creativity. It's
something known, rigorous and logical; there are
clear specifications that you can meet. You are
making good use of your time when you meet the
technological specifications.

On the other hand, if your requirements are
in the creative, non-routine realm, then you are
making good use of your time when you do not im-
pose any technological limitations on your use of
the time. All the requirements are for freedom.
You are by definition in an area that is exploring
the unknown. And if you don't know the answers to
the questions you are dealing with, you obviously
also don't know the answer to how long it is going
to take to deal with them or how you can best use
your time to get to the solution. So when people
make technological demands on time in a creative
milieu, it is terrible. In our educational system
we do it to an absurd degree. We even have
"creativity tests." They have become a standard
part of the educational testing repertoire.

With a dual concept of time, I think we can
start coming to grips with the anxieties of parents and enrollees regarding the use of time in
the school. The point is this: to the extent that

somebody in the school seeks to do something that
is known and well defined, then this should be
carried out with dispatch. We've always stood for
that. For example, consider the way we have run
our school. We have never allowed the school to
be run in a lackadaisical manner. We never said,
"Somebody, sometime will come up with a way to
answer the mail; let it stack up till this happens." We collect the mail and answer it every
day, using a specified procedure designed by the
School Meeting and the Office Clerk, and it gets
done. There is a specified way to answer the
phone, and a specified way to clean the school,
and take care of the grounds. Insofar as the
school deals with known things, we have always
stood for dealing with them through a technological use of time. The same has always been part of
our attitude toward enrollees. If anyone says
they want technical training in using a certain
tool, for example in learning how to type, we
don't sit them in front of a typewriter and tell
them to be creative. It is interesting to note
how the new "creative" approach to education dif-
fers from us. What do "progressive educators" do
with children and typewriters? They sit them in
front of the machines, and they play around, and
eventually they are supposed to develop a "positive" attitude toward typing and somehow, somewhere along the line, someone will sneak in typing
lessons. In our school, if somebody says they
want to learn how to type, we throw a typing
manual at them and say, "sit down and practice."
There is one way to type, the standard touch
system, and you practice it fifteen minutes a day
for several months until you get enough speed and
it's automatic. Period. So that's one half the
answer. A parent comes up and says, "Is my child
going to make good use of his time?" Half of the

answer is, "If your children are going to want to make a technological use of their time, then they will find that the school's approach is going to be technological." Our attitude will be that they should do it efficiently. We are not going to try to fool them into wasting their time about it and doing it in a roundabout way.

On the other hand, the answer to the other half of the question is quite different. If the student doesn't have a technological goal -- if they say, for example, that they want to get themselves together to find out what they want to do in life, that they want to work out what their relationship is to themselves, to their parents, to the culture -- these are the non-technological aspects of life, and to these there is only one good use of time, a non-technological one. You can't say to a person in that position, "We will give you three months to figure out your attitude toward life," or "We will let you come here for a year, and if after a year you can pull yourself together, then we will let you come again; if not, it's been a waste of time and money."

It should be clear that the only situation where one can be subjected to a time deadline is a technological situation. If a person comes here to learn to do woodworking, and if we know that a normal apprenticeship in woodworking takes a year, then we can be tested on that. And if the person doesn't come out a woodworker because we are dragging our feet and not providing the tools or instruction, then we have failed. By the same token, if the student poses a question that is not routine, we have got to make it clear that the answer is not going to be routine. The only possible good use of time in that case is not to consider time at all in the process.

In summary, I think that somehow it has got
to be clear that we recognize in this school the
dual sides of the culture. We respect them both.
We don't scorn the technological side of time when
it's applied to technological uses. On the other
hand, we do not make routine demands in the area
of creative work; parents mustn't and students
themselves mustn't either. Only if we recognize
this dichotomy, only when we give each aspect of
time its due, will we be able to give a clear
answer to the question, "When do people make good
use of their time in the school?"

Snapshots

Hanna Greenberg

People often ask me why I love to spend my time at the Sudbury Valley School. Following are three vignettes that are good examples of the kind of relationships that the adults and children develop over the years.

1. This happened a long time ago but is still fresh in my memory. The person in question, age ten or so, was punished for some mischief he caused after hours. He was not allowed to stay in the building after 5:00 p.m. and so was obliged to wait for his ride outside. On the day of the incident I was closing school and doing the trash. At 5:00 he asked me for special dispensation to stay indoors because it was raining. Being both pragmatic and soft-hearted, I said, "I will let you stay if you help with the trash." He replied: "I would help you with the trash but I don't be-lieve in bribery, so I will wait outside."

2. I was talking to three little kids about five years old. One said, "Oh, Hanna, you are so nice, you are my favorite staff member." Then another said, "Not mine. I love Joan the best." After the first shock, I felt very flattered that the child felt comfortable enough to tell me the truth, so I ventured to ask her, "I thought you like Marge a lot?" She answered, "Oh yes, I like

Marge better than you too, but Joan is my favorite."

3.   One teenager asked me to teach an algebra
class.   I replied that I had never taught algebra
before and was not sure if I could teach it well.
She said to me, "I think that you should do it
with us.   This way you will learn and next time
you will know how to do it.   Won't that make you
feel good?"   Of course I am teaching algebra and
we all enjoy it very much.

I like to spend my days with people who are
honest and vital, whose hearts are filled with
love and optimism.

* * * * *

One of the things I enjoy most about working
at SVS is the conversations I have with students
and sometimes parents.   Sometimes a kid will say
something in two sentences that I have been trying
to articulate for years and spend hours talking
about.

One girl, aged about ten, had a hard time
adjusting to the school.   She wanted to be here,
but it was clear to us and to her parents that the
going was rough.   We, the adults, thought that she
missed her old friends, or perhaps felt shy.   It
turned out to be nothing of the sort.

Here is what she said: "In my other school,
they showed you things and you did them, but here
you get an empty canvas and you have to fill it
yourself with your life."

Now I have tried to explain for years that we
feel that each child has a different way of learning, has different needs, different talents, etc.,
but this little girl said it better than I ever
did -- and I am glad to report that she is filling
her canvas very beautifully.

Sudbury Valley's Secret Weapon: Allowing People of Different Ages to Mix Freely at School

Daniel Greenberg

For a long time I had the strong conviction that age mixing, which is one of the most obvious feature of Sudbury Valley, is among the most important educational components of the school (as well as being required by its democratic principles). But whenever I tried to explain it, I couldn't quite put into words why I felt that it played such a central role in the way children learn and develop. Recently however I had an experience that galvanized the entire concept for me. Not that the experience itself was especially unique but, as I will soon relate, it had certain characteristics that finally put all the pieces rather abruptly into place. Perhaps the best thing is to relate the experience first, and then go back and trace my thinking from the beginning.

What happened was simply that I was present when a play group was being organized for children about three years old. A bunch of three year olds were playing around in and out of the house of one

of the parents, and my own three year old was one
of them.

What I saw was a lot of activity, but almost
all of it individual activity. The children were
apparently playing together, except that when you
looked closely you saw that what was happening was
that they were obviously enjoying each others'
company and that they were interested in being
near each other, but they were playing together
separately. Each one was riding his own pedal car
or tricycle and making a lot of noise and looking
toward the other, but there was no joint activity,
nothing in which they collaborated was taking
place. Also, there was a lot of noise. There was
also one other feature that is pervasive in nur-
sery schools, though I must say very few observers
mention it. A lot of the activity was markedly
repetitious, rutted. Somebody would ride back and
forth, back and forth, with a big smile on his
face, and somebody would sing for an inordinate
length of time, always the same thing. Interestingly the most repetitious activities were those
of children who were doing it in each other's
presence. Whereas the child who might be staying
completely alone in a different part of the house
would be doing something original and varied. All
these kinds of activity are very common to all
such groups, but for some reason the events of
this particular day triggered a train of thought
in my mind that made many things fall into place.
So let me proceed with some more general observations.

If you look around at society at large, or
any segment of it, you cannot fail to notice that
segregation by age, or by skill, or by ability, is
not a prevalent phenomenon. Adults pay very
little attention to these factors when they interact with other adults. Whether you are looking at

a business or a store or a university or whatever, the adult population is most diverse: there are some people on the verge of retirement, some in their forties, some in their twenties just start-ing out, and they all are participating together in the enterprise. I know of no enterprise that has the kind of segregation that is common in schools.

Indeed, if you think about this matter as it applies to society at large, it starts to give you some insight about what's going on in educational institutions. In the everyday institutions popu-lated by adults, it is generally accepted that it's a good thing if there's a lot of contact and communication between people who have different degrees of experience in life and different deg-rees of ability in their work. It's a good thing for the enterprise. It's something beneficial. If people thought it was better for such inter-mingling not to happen, they would prevent it from happening.

Now, I suspect that most people simply accept this because that's what they're used to, and that very few people who run businesses or enterprises of any kind have thought through why they let people mix freely; that's the way it has always been and that's the way it is. But whether or not people know why it is good, it is a common feature of our rather successful society, and it is this fact that I want to file as background for later reference.

Let us proceed to the central point: What is it that goes on when a child grows up and learns how to cope with the world? I think it is rather broadly agreed that the essence of the process of maturation is the development by the child of the ability to form a world view; to come to grips with the world; to solve problems; somehow to find

a place in the world; to get enough of a sense of
identity to be able to interact with the world.
There are many different ways of saying it.
Basically, growing up is acquiring the ability to
cope with the surroundings, rather than acquiring
a set of static abilities that you live with the
rest of your life. Modern thinkers tend to see
life as an ongoing interaction between an organism
and the world around it. Life is not something
that takes on a set form when you become an adult
and then just plays itself out; that is more typical of the view held in the past. Now, life is
viewed much more as a process. To reach maturation means that you finally attain the ability,
more or less, to go on coping day after day, year
after year, in a creative, successful, imaginative
way, with the ever-changing world surrounding you.
The difference between a mature person and an
immature person is that an immature person still
is lacking much of this ability, still has trouble
getting a handle on things. The mature person
supposedly has developed the ability to find ways
of dealing with the world around him, solving the
problems it presents, and creating structures
within which he can function.

Since adulthood is an ongoing process of
dealing with the world, learning and development
can be seen to be the acquirement of the skills
needed to be an adult. The focus is therefore on
becoming a successful problem solver and builder
of models of reality. A successful adult is a
person who can do these things well, can take a
problem, think about it, analyze it, and somehow
come up with a solution that is valid within his
model of reality. To function successfully
throughout life he has to have the ability to
build models that make sense out of reality for
him.

Given this view of what the process of life is, the question of education -- or of childhood in general -- is how does a child develop the ability to do these things, and what is the best educational environment in which to develop these skills? How do you become a good problem solver? How do you become a good model builder?

One of the ways is by studying the responses of other people in situations similar to the ones you are in. A person learns not only by making everything up from scratch himself, but by looking around and observing and studying and thinking about how other people deal with the world. That's where age mixing comes in. A person who grows up absolutely alone in a totally isolated environment is obviously going to have a completely different way of functioning as an adult than a person who has grown up in a social environment. Indeed, one of the functions of social interactions in a society is to provide alternate life models for the people in the society to study constantly.

Now, when you are an adult, you know this. You are constantly looking around at your colleagues, peers, neighbors, etc. I'm not talking about "followers" or authority-worshippers. Even -- or especially -- the most highly original and creative adult is constantly looking around him at other people and wondering how they approach things, or what they see in life; and he is constantly striving to learn from these alternative models, and to integrate them into his world view in order to use them somehow for his own benefit.

What is true of adults is doubly true of children. A child, who doesn't yet have the skills for coping on his own, looks at alternative models around him not only to see what they are,

but to educate himself into the very mechanisms of
model building.

That's a rather intricate second-order
concept. Let me see if I can make it clearer with
some examples. Say I'm studying physics. As a
practicing physicist I will be interested in what
other practicing physicists do in order to see
what kind of theories they use, what kind of formulas they apply to a given situation, what sort
of experiments they design and so forth. But when
a child gets interested in a physics problem he
looks at what others are doing not primarily to
find out what kinds of theories and formulas they
will apply to a situation, but to learn what kind
of thought processes are involved in physics.
What manner of problem solving is physics?
There's a real distinction here. The distinction
is between, on the one hand, knowing what physics
is about and looking around you to see what kind
of physics other people are doing and, on the
other hand, trying to find out what physics is
about.

This is just an example of what is going on
all the time with a developing child. Unfortunately this is a distinction that has been
missed in the educational literature, even by
people who write about process and problem solving. The child is not ready to learn simply how
to solve problems. He has to learn first the
fundamental frameworks within which the kind of
problem solving adults do takes place. What is
the nature of physics? What is the nature of
biological thought? What is the nature of historical analysis? The developing child with an
interest in politics is not first and foremost
concerned with distinguishing between how different politicians deal with problems. That is the
concern of adults. But the child is trying first

to comprehend how politicians approach problems in
the first place. What is the nature of the political thought process? Until he has a grasp on
what goes into making a political decision he is
not going to be able to think about whether A is
a better solution than B.

     This subtle difference is the key to every-
thing. The child is trying to understand the
nature of model building, the nature of problem
solving, the nature of the process of life. He's
not simply concerned with weighing alternate
models and alternate approaches. It's a second
order problem that the child has. That's the key
to what's wrong with the way our present schools
segregate by age or ability.

     There are two extreme situations that a child
can be in, each of which is a poor situation for
learning. One extreme is that the child is limited to being only with adults. For example, the
Mark Hopkins ideal, one child with one adult on
the opposite end of the log. Here you have the
generation gap with a vengeance. The adult is an
adult already; he is exploring a wide variety of
problem solving techniques, world models and so
forth. And if he is really a mature, intelligent,
well-developed person, he will be really adept at
it, constantly weighing alternatives and coming up
with creative new ideas. The child, by contrast,
has a very poorly formed idea of how to go about
these processes, as I have said. So here he is,
stuck with his adult partner, and the adult
doesn't begin to understand why the child is
having such a hard time. The adult may really be
interested in the child, trying constantly to
explain what he's doing. The more the adult
explains to the child what he's doing, the less
the child understands. Because the child's
problem is that he doesn't have a common line of

communication with the adult. They are not talking on the same level.

Any adult who has spent a lot of time talking
to children will have these frustrations. This is
the chief problem in teaching any subject. For
instance, you get a bunch of freshman college
physics students and then you put a college professor in with them, and the college professor may
be just as patient as ever, explaining the same
material fifty-eight times. But the problem isn't
that the student doesn't understand the words, or
has trouble copying them down. The problem is
that the freshman doesn't understand what the
physicist's way of approaching the world is. No
matter how many times the teacher repeats a
particular physical theory, it is lacking any
foundation in the world view of the student. So
there's no communication and nothing every happens
in the student's mind. That is such a common
phenomenon that it's pathetic. It's not a generation gap because of age; it's a question of talking at two different levels. You can be the best
pedagogue in the world. You can try every trick.
But you never really get around it. Ultimately
what happens in that kind of situation is that the
child ultimately grows up. Which means that he
ultimately somehow creates in his own mind an idea
of what it is that the physicist is doing. In
some cases this can be a very fantastic idea. You
do get people who have the most bizarre notions of
what history or physics or philosophy or any other
subject is about. When you look into it a little,
you usually find out that they have such bizarre
notions because of the gap I have just described
between them and their mentors throughout their
youth. In fact, this happens very often with
people who have grown up in families with highly
intellectual parents. The children often come up

with the strangest notions precisely because the
parents have been "wonderful" parents, explaining
things year after year, and the children never
really caught on.

The other extreme that is equally destructive
to a normal mental development is segregating
children, for example by age. This essentially
means putting all children together who are at the
same level of development. Nowadays this is done
with a vengeance in schools; educators are no
longer satisfied with grade levels that are determined by age. If you simply determine grades by
age you don't really get children grouped according to their developmental level, so most modern
educators have a whole series of tests to enable
them to put everybody together at the same developmental age. And they consider this a great step
forward.

That's even more cruel to a child because
here everybody is in the same trouble and nobody
can help each other out. They don't even have the
benefit of any successful models around them.
They have to try to find out how to develop the
ability and the skill and the framework and the
methodology of coping with the world on their
own. They are at a double disadvantage.

Now what people do in regular school is
combine the two cruel extremes. Neither extreme
happens very often by itself, but in the schools
we make the combination of the extremes happen
regularly. In other words, the way this society's
educational system is conceived is to take a bunch
of children who are at the same developmental age,
and then stick them in a room together with an
adult. This combines the worst features of both
situations. On the one hand everybody is at a
loss, because all they see is the adult and they
don't learn from the adult anything about the

second order processes. On the other hand when
they turn around and try to get help from their
neighbor they can't because the neighbor is in the
same boat as they are. So it's the most frustrating possible situation. And that to me is the
key, that phrase "the most frustrating situation."

The psychological manifestations that occur
in schools and in play groups or whatever are
almost textbook manifestations of frustration.
What happens when you are terribly frustrated?
For one thing, you become angry. Anybody who
walks into any school immediately feels a tremendous amount of unspecific anger and hostility.
The unspecific nature of the hostility is
crucial. They are not angry at a social wrong;
theirs is not a rational anger, because something
specific happened that they are upset about.
Rather, they are overwhelmed by an unspecific
anger directed abroad in a scattershot fashion.

The companion to this anger is unspecific
anxiety. Not anxiety because your mother just
left and you don't know when she'll come back,
which is specific anxiety and rationally based.
In unspecific anxiety, you are anxious, but you
don't know why. Frustration is just the kind of
thing that produces unspecific anxiety. And if
you are frustrated about problem solving, you are
frustrated at the most fundamental level of your
mental process. You just can't get a handle on
the things that your mind wants to do most of all,
namely, to solve problems and build models. You
are not managing to do it, you are not getting any
help from your colleagues, who are in the same
boat, nor from your teachers, who can't reach
you. And you are just plain frustrated at not
making adequate progress.

Unspecific hostility. Unspecific anxiety.
And the third manifestation is what I will call

incipient autism. By this I mean the beginning of
inward-turning, the creation of a barrier of
alienation from the rest of the world. Behavior
that manifests itself in early years as rutted,
routine, repeated behavior that follows a set
pattern time and again. The difference between
the early years and the later years is that in the
early years the motor responses haven't yet been
suppressed. So that early incipient autism often
shows itself as routine motor behavior. Later, as
society manages to control this kind of behavior,
it gets shut down. "Don't yell." "Don't run
around." "Don't make a lot of noise." So by the
time we come around to a slightly later age, the
same category of behavior becomes a dulled
turning-off.

These, then, are three characteristics that,
I submit, are very widespread in groups that are
segregated by age or developmental level. All
three arise from the frustration of not being able
to get a handle on things.

You just don't see that kind of behavior in
children who feel that they can deal with their
surroundings. You see precisely the opposite --
exuberant activity, eagerness to get on with the
job, eagerness to go on to the next thing. Which
brings me around pretty much to the point of the
whole thing. Having talked about the two bad
extremes and their combination as presently found
in the regular schools, I think that it is obvious
why I think that free age mixing is such a critical factor at Sudbury Valley. It is the key to
everything else. Free age mixing provides a free
flow of interaction among people at different
points along the maturation process. It enables
you, as you are growing toward adulthood, always
to find somebody in both directions. You can find
somebody who is just a few steps ahead in learning

how to deal with the environment (just a <u>few</u> steps
ahead, and therefore not so far ahead that he is
no longer encountering a lot of the same problems). Somebody who still speaks the same language, who still makes a lot of the same mistakes. But at the same time, he has achieved a
few of the things that you want to achieve, and
since you can talk about 80% of it rather easily
(because you are in the same boat for 80% of it),
the other 20% becomes an awful lot easier to
understand. On the other hand, it is equally
important to be able to turn around and find
somebody a little behind you. Because you get a
handle on your accomplishments and on your maturation by refining them through explaining and re-
explaining and making it clear to somebody who is
asking you. This is the real meaning of the commonplace saying that teaching and learning are two
sides of the same coin. They are indeed. It is
equally important to have solved a problem and
also to be able to verbalize the solution and hone
it against somebody who is quizzing you and giving
you a hard time about it. And that's what you get
when you're able to look to one side and find
somebody who is a year or two older than you, and
then to the other side and find somebody a year or
two younger.

Actually, at Sudbury Valley, a careful study
of inter-age contacts would probably yield the
classic bell-shaped statistical curve representing
the distribution of contacts between the persons
at different stages of development. The likelihood is that for the most part children will be
communicating with others who are within a narrow
range on either side of them, and progressively
less time -- but <u>some</u> time -- with people farther
and farther away from them on either side. The
distant contacts definitely exist, and they serve

to accelerate the normal developmental process.
Every now and then a person can take a big step
very easily. The little steps take up most of the
time, but age mixing also allows you to take a lot
of very surprising and unpredictable big steps.
We find this happening all the time. Suddenly a
child of a certain age will hit it off fantast-
ically with somebody five or six years older, or
younger. We used to be amazed at this, for
example when teenagers would suddenly find real

satisfaction out of relating to very young kids.
This has nothing to do with maternal or paternal
instincts. Rather, this has to do with their
finding tremendous value in following through a
big step taken across a wide gulf. And just as
often, a young child will make a leap in some area
and find a common language with somebody who is
developmentally way ahead in a certain area.

A lot of people have remarked on the absence
of significant cliques at Sudbury Valley. There
are friendships, and there are mini-groups, but
real cliques are very rare in this school. Since
cliques are one of the most common characteristics
of ordinary school situations, their relative
absence here is all the more remarkable. What
accounts for the state of affairs here? The
answer is simple: even when you have a group of
friends with whom you like to spend most of your
time, there is always somebody outside of that
group with whom you want to spend some of your
time. There is always somebody who has an interest that runs parallel to yours in some other
area. As a result, you find children constantly
turning outside of their most immediate friendship
group in order to develop some area that they
don't share in common with others. Hence, there
are no fixed cliques.

Another thing that I think is remarkable in
the Sudbury Valley School, and directly related to
free age mixing, is the noticeable absence of
preening and showing off. Of course, I don't mean
to say that it doesn't happen; after all, ours is
a society practically indoctrinated to show off.
But when you look at the school you can't help but
noting how high a percentage of the interactions
do not have showing off, or even jealousy, as one
of their prime characteristics. Why?

The answer is directly related to age mixing. Showing off, and jealousy, is practically forced upon people trapped in a narrow age group; it's a matter of establishing the pecking order of the group. You are all in the same boat, and so all that's left to you is to fight with each other to establish physical or psychological supremacy. At Sudbury Valley, a lot of the point is taken out of it. I mean, who are you going to show off to? What's the point of it? I'm not talking here in moral terms. I'm talking about what in fact happens in the learning interactions. Here, everybody knows and is quick to acknowledge that everybody is ignorant. For example, what would be the point of a child showing off that he knows how to read well? He knows that he can't read as well as a person three or four years older, with whom he is constantly interacting. Age mixing takes away the necessity to show off, because age mixing is predicated on the healthy human motivation of learning from any available source. A person who is healthy will always want to learn from whomever there is around who can teach him anything that will help him develop. And his satisfaction is gotten from accomplishment, not from preening.

I would like to end by returning to where I started. Everything that I said as applied to school age children becomes extremely vivid when you see it in three year olds. Three year olds are still in a very rudimentary stage of developing their basic communication skills. Now if you can't even communicate easily with the other person, your frustration level is redoubled. Because not only are you all in the same boat, but you can't even talk to each other in the same boat. So what you have is a bunch of children who can't even express to each other that they want to do the things that they are capable of doing

together; they can't even express to each other
that they want to do things on their own level.
They know what they want to do, they have a
picture of it, but they can't get the message
through. So when there are just three year olds
together and not a lot of other children around to
help them, there are no bridges in the communication among them.

There we were, sitting together, a bunch of
three year olds and a bunch of adults. The adults
couldn't cross this communication gap because, as
I have explained, there was no way I could effectively talk with another three year old whom I
never met before. He didn't trust me. He didn't
know me. I didn't understand him. He didn't
understand me. It was unbearable. However, had
there been a few four or five year olds in there,
the whole picture would have been different.
Those problems would not have occurred. They
could have communicated to the four years olds.
The four year olds would have been the bridge.
Older children are well known to be the perfect
bridge of communication among little children, and
between little children and adults.

The free age mixing at the Sudbury Valley
School has to be somehow explained to people who
come and observe what we're doing. I'm afraid
this is a very hard task, because the general
educational system is so polarized in the opposite
direction. But it is important for us to do
because, in purely educational terms, we reap very
important educational benefits from this age
mixing. It greatly hastens the maturation and
development of the children who are in the school,
especially those who have started young.

In a way, this is noticed by many people who
visit. They remark on the result without understanding one of the major causes. They will

remark on the fact that it is amazing that our
ten, eleven, twelve, and thirteen year olds are so
developed, so mature. Adults are able to communicate with them and talk to them, which means that
they are much farther along in becoming comparable
to adults in their model building and problem
solving abilities than ten, eleven, or twelve year
olds are in the society at large. As I see it,
this is a direct result of the effect that free
age mixing has on the children at this school.

The Beech Tree

Hanna Greenberg

On a glorious morning this Fall I "saw" the
beech tree for the first time. That seems an
amazing statement coming from a person who has
been at SVS for eighteen years -- amazing, but
true. Like everyone else, I have seen the tree in
the Fall when its leaves turn red and are then
shed, letting the branches show their magnificent
structure throughout the Winter. I have also
witnessed a new growth of Spring when the budding
leaves give the tree a pink halo and slowly turn
to their deep green color. I have also seen
generation after generation of little children
learn to climb the mighty tree, going higher and
higher, sometimes reaching its crown and perching
there for hours. But it was only the other week
that I really "saw" the tree, really understood
it. Being an adult, I did not know how to truly
experience the tree, until a little girl taught me
how. This is what happened.

One day, Naomi, her face beaming, announced
to me (like many little ones before her) that she
finally is able to climb into the beech tree all
by herself. She said that Alison had taught her
how, and now she would show me. I went out with
her because I wanted to share her joy and because
the morning was so brilliant with vivid colors and
luxuriant sunlight shimmering in the dew on the

red and yellow leaves. Naomi showed me how she
climbed and came down, and then told me to follow
suit. Now, I had helped scores of children get up
and many more to get down when they felt stuck,
but I had never attempted to climb the tree myself. Naomi does not take "no" readily, and I
knew that if I was to retain her respect for me, I
just had to perform for her! She very patiently
and clearly showed me, step by step, how to climb
up and how to get down, and I did it for the first
time ever.

When I got up to the first level I was struck
by the beauty of the perch. I am not able to
describe the mighty branches, the cozy space or
the feelings of awe that overcame me. Suffice it
to say that I realized that I had "seen" the tree
for the first time. We adults think of ourselves
as knowledgable, and of our children as needing to
learn and to be taught, but in this case I'd bet
that any kid at SVS would be amazed at our ignorance and insensitivity to the grandeur that is
there for us to see and is ignored. Naomi was a
good teacher and I will always be grateful for
what she taught me.

On the Nature of Sports at S.V.S. and the Limitations of Language in Describing S.V.S. to the World

Michael Greenberg

Have you ever noticed the uniqueness of the
way that sports are played at S.V.S.?

The experience is a beautiful one which
brings out most of the noble characteristics which
a person can possess. It also illustrates a point
about language and the S.V.S. experience that is
worth thinking about; for, although we give our
activities at the school the same names as activities that take place elsewhere (for instance,
"soccer games" or "history class"), what is actually happening during those activities at school
is so fundamentally different from what happens
elsewhere that the name becomes misleading. This
is why it seems impossible, at times, to explain
the school to people who haven't actually seen it.

To describe the school, we must explain what
actually happens, mentally and physically, step by
step, because people have no <u>direct</u> experience
that is the same as ours. At best, their idealis-
tic, utopian ideas may resemble our day to day
experiences at school. People can be reached by

showing them how their ideals of freedom and responsibility, of democracy and fair justice, trans-
late into day to day actions. We know that people
in other schools have no direct experience of
these things. What we forget is that, even after
school, most people don't have a direct experience
of true democracy, fair justice, freedom, and responsibility in the full sense that we know them at
S.V.S. just as people in other countries have no
idea of what day to day life is like in the U.S.A.
through reading the Constitution and the Bill of
Rights.

Which brings me to how utterly incomplete and
misleading terms like "soccer game" and "history
class" are in describing those activities at
S.V.S. I will take soccer as an example.

In other schools soccer is a game where all
players on a team are of a similar age, sex, and,
if the school is big enough, ability. It is
played at designated times selected by the
school. It is highly competitive both as regards
an individual's performance on the team and the
performance of team against team. There is a lot
of peer pressure and one's status and sense of
worth is highly dependent on physical performance. The fact that people manage to have some
fun in spite of all these negative aspects says a
lot about the deep human satisfaction that arises
out of physical exertion and play.

This is what usually happens in other
schools. The players arrive at the designated
time wearing their uniforms. They are told by
their coach how to improve their performances (not
how to have more fun). They go to their designated positions. A team will always have more
players than are allowed on the field so the
people who don't perform as well as others will
not be allowed to spend as much time playing.

They play the game. "They 'work' the game" might
be a more appropriate phrase, because traditional,
organized amateur sport is almost as regimented as
professional sports.

People who are paid $200,000 a year to beat
other people in sports should be performance
oriented. The average person who simply wants to
enjoy the physical process of play, or who wants
to improve his own ability to kick a ball simply
as an athletic challenge, should be enjoyment
oriented, not process oriented.

Here is what happens at an S.V.S. soccer
game. One person says, "Let's play soccer" to
some other people. Whoever feels like playing at
that moment comes to the field. There are six
year olds, 10 year olds, 18 year olds, maybe a
staff member or parent who feels like joining in.
There are boys and girls. Teams are then chosen
with a conscious effort at creating evenly matched
sides. Someone who hasn't been there would not
believe the amount of effort that goes into making
the teams even. Given the diversity of the players, this often consists of one team having an
extra "big kid" who can play well and the other
team getting a small army of six year olds to get
in his way. People want even teams because they
are playing for fun. It's no fun to play a game
with lopsided teams.

After a game starts, someone will often come
and say, "Can I play too?" and the teams will be
rearranged to accommodate them, trading players
back and forth. If that proves impossible, they
will be told "Get someone equal to you to play
also." The game is played by whomever wants to
play, for as long as they feel like playing.
There will always be certain people who value
winning, but there is little peer performance
pressure. Most people don't really care who wins.

Now, you might get the impression that people
are not trying very hard to be good at the game,
but that's not true. Because the process of play
is only fun if you exert effort and challenge
yourself. That is why people developed the idea
of games like soccer in the first place. Running
around for no reason gets boring, but running
around trying to kick a ball between two posts
that are guarded by people who are trying to stop
you -- that's exciting.

The people who play sports as we do at
S.V.S. learn far more profound lessons about life
than those that can be taught by regimented,
performance-oriented sports. They learn teamwork

-- not the "we against them" type of teamwork,
but the teamwork of a diverse group of people of
diverse talents organizing themselves to pursue a
common activity -- the teamwork of life. They
learn excellence, not the "I'm a star" type of
excellence, but the type of excellence that comes
from setting a standard for yourself to live up to
and then trying your best to live up to it.

I'm 23 years old and I've played a lot of
soccer. It would be pretty silly for me to try to
be better than the three 8 year olds who crowd
around my feet every time I try to kick the ball.
I think that the 8 year olds are too busy running
after kids who are three feet taller than they are
to worry about being the best 8 year old. In this
game, as in real life, the only standard that
matters is one you set for yourself. One of the
profound truths you learn is that we are all so
different from each other that peer pressure and
comparisons of worth are meaningless. If you're
11 years old and you are only allowed to play with
other 11 year olds, it's very hard to glimpse this
profound truth which unlocks the true meaning of
excellence.

They learn responsibility and restraint. In
all the years of playing very physical games like
football, soccer, and basketball, there has never
been an injury beyond a minor cut or bruise.
People play all these sports in their regular
clothes without any of the standard protective
equipment that is normally required. How can this
be explained when people wearing protective pads
regularly injure each other with alarming frequen-
cy? Because in a regimented, performance-oriented
way of looking at sports (or life), making sure
you don't hurt someone becomes less important than
winning. So it doesn't matter how much you talk
about "sportsmanship" or how many safety pads you

wear, people will get hurt. When you approach
sports (or life) as a fun, exciting process, as
something that is done for the sheer joy and
beauty of doing it, then not hurting someone, not
impairing their ability to enjoy the same process
becomes a top priority.

This whole experience of sports at the school
is just one of the many ways in which the kids
answer the question, "What activities produce a
meaningful life?" or, to put it more simply, "What
is the meaning of life?" For people at school,
freedom is not just a tremendous wonder, it is
also a tremendous burden. This freedom to do what
you want forces you to decide what you want.
People play because they are free to, they want
to, and they are alive. At the school, sport and
physical play are magnificent expressions of the
people who play them.

To participate in an activity where the clash
of unequal bodies is transformed through teamwork,
pursuit of person excellence, responsibility and
restraint into a common union of equal souls in
pursuit of meaningful experience has been one of
the most profound experiences of my life. I am
sure it has had a similar effect on others. This
can be easy for anyone to understand, but not if I
simply tell them that I "played a lot of soccer at
school."

When I was 8 years old and people asked me
what I did with my time at S.V.S., I said,
"Nothing." I now realize what I meant to say was
"everything." Education is not so much a matter
of learning facts as it is a matter of learning
how to think. What the school teaches (or,
rather, allows people to learn) is how to think.
It does this by allowing people to talk, listen,
play and contemplate as they see fit. It is this

rare and wonderful privilege that colors and gives
meaning to every activity.

The language that we use to describe the
school must take into account the uniqueness of
the context within which things happen here. We
must speak the language of philosophy. We must
talk about the processes that occur when one of
the deepest needs of the human spirit, the need
for freedom, is fulfilled: the process that occurs
when a young mind is forced by that freedom to
find activities which it considers meaningful
(because humans hate to be bored); the process
that occurs when you do things because you want
to, not because someone or something makes you.
This is not a school to be compared blandly with
other schools. It is a way of thinking and of
living.

How the School is Governed; Who Cares?

Daniel Greenberg

I thought you might like to know how the
school is run.

Actually, you probably wouldn't, if you're
like most people. That sobering fact came as
something of a disappointment to us many years
ago, after we had spent countless hours singly, in
various groups, with lawyers, etc. over a period
of years, all for the noble purpose of setting up
a system of government inbred with lofty ideals
and profound political principles. We never tired
of refining our thoughts, and we still continue to
do so. At first, we thought everyone else was
just as interested in these matters. It didn't
take us long to find out they weren't.

Anyway, when you think about it, it's not all
that surprising. Most everybody in this country
is ferociously committed to the fundamental principles on which our nation has been founded, as
they understand these principles. But how many
people have the foggiest notion of the details of
government? Do you know the various functions of
the Town Meeting, the Moderator, the Standing
Committees, the Selectmen, the County Government,
the Regional Water and School Districts, the State
Government and Agencies, the Federal Government
and Agencies, the District Court, Superior Court,
Supreme Court, Court of Appeals, Land Court,

Maritime Court, Tax Court, Federal District Court,
etc., etc., etc.? For most of our lives we get
along fine without any idea of what all these arms
of governance do. When we occasionally run afoul
of them, or need them, we get a quick education.

Well, I just thought you might be curious
about the school. If you aren't, stop reading.
If you are, I'll take you through a short thumbnail sketch of how we operate.

The school as a legal entity is a Massachusetts Corporation, The Sudbury Valley School,
Inc. Because it is a non-profit corporation,
there are no shareholders. Instead, the Corporation consists of the school's Assembly which,
under the by-laws, is made up of students, staff,
parents, trustees, and specially elected public
members. (You can get a copy of the By-laws by
asking in the office.) The Assembly meets regularly once a year, in the late Spring, and determines all the school's basic policies, the annual
budget, salary scales, tuition, the award of dip-
lomas, and the Officers and Trustees. The agenda
of the Assembly is published in advance and mailed
to all members. Any Assembly member can put an
item on the agenda by mailing it to the Secretary
of the Corporation, c/o the office; items (with a
few exceptions) can also be brought up on the
floor of the meeting for discussion and vote.

The Officers of the Corporation are a Presi-
dent, who presides at meetings of the Assembly and
Trustees, and whose most important power is that
of calling special meetings when he sees fit; a
Treasurer and a Secretary, both of whose functions
are the standard ones implied by their titles.

Every year the Assembly also elects a Board
of Trustees which, unlike virtually all other
schools and corporations, in our case has no <u>power</u>
at all. Rather, the Board is our advisory panel,

studying as best it can the various questions
referred to it by the Assembly and reporting back
to the Assembly when it is ready to do so.   The
number of Trustees is currently limited by the
By-laws to a maximum of twenty.   As a matter of
tradition, Trustees meetings are open to all
Assembly members to attend and, where possible,
advance notice is given of the topic under
discussion.

The day-to-day life of the school is governed
by the School Meeting, both directly and through
its various agents.

The School Meeting consists of all the people
at school on a day-to-day basis -- namely, all
students and staff, each of whom has a vote.   (As
a practical matter, students greatly outnumber the
staff.   This really keeps the staff on its tocs.
Any staff member wishing to promote a particular
scheme has to have his facts and arguments carefully honed to convince a majority of those present and voting, most of whom are usually students.)   The School Meeting meets every Thursday
at 1:00 PM.   The meetings are run efficiently and
formally according to strict rules of order, with
a fixed order of agenda.   The agenda is always
published in advance and is called the School
Meeting Record.

The School Meeting has full operational
authority to run the school, subject only to the
policies set forth by the Assembly.   The School
Meeting does it all: it spends the money, hires
(and fires) the staff, passes all the school rules
(the permanent rules are codified in the School
Meeting Law Book which can be obtained through the
office), oversees discipline, and sets up all
sorts of administrative entities to keep things
running smoothly.   It is presided over by the
School Meeting Chairman who is effectively the

school's Chief Executive Officer. In the early
years, the Chairman was almost always a staff
member, but since 1973 Chairpersons have been
students. The School Meeting also elects a
Secretary to keep records.

School Meetings are open (except on rare
occasions; they are closed, for example, when
there is a personal discussion involving a particular student). You should attend one some day
-- it is the heart of the school and is an amazing
institution to observe.

To keep all the myriad activities of the
school running smoothly, the School Meeting
creates Clerks, Committees, and School Corporations. (These are all spelled out in detail in
the Law Book and in a Management Manual kept in
the office.)

Clerks are basically administrative officers. For example, there is an Attendance Clerk
who supervises attendance records, after-hours use
of the building, keys, etc. There is a Grounds
Clerk who takes care of the grounds, a Building
Maintenance Clerk who takes care of the buildings,
and so on. When the School Meeting creates a
Clerkship, it spells out the officer's exact
powers and duties and confers its authority on the
Clerk within the domain it has defined.

Committees take care of broader tasks. For
example, the Aesthetics Committee takes care of
all matters relating to the school's appearance,
interior and exterior design, furnishings,
exhibits/art work, cleanliness.

School Corporations are formal interest
groups. They are Sudbury Valley's equivalent of
Departments at other schools. For example, there
is a Woodworking Corporation which takes care of
all woodworking activities; a Photolab Corporation; and so forth. Corporations are chartered

for a specific set of purposes by the School Meeting and given certain powers. Funds are channeled through the Corporations to support various educational activities. The great advantage School Corporations have over Departments is that the former can be formed and disbanded according to the needs and interests of the students, while the latter, unlike old soldiers, never die or fade away, but just keep rolling along. (I was once associated with a Physics Department at a prestigious women's college that occupied half a floor of a four-story building, even though there were no physics majors any more -- it was just a left-over from fifty years earlier!)

The school's disciplinary problems are taken care of in the context of the Judicial System established by the School Meeting. (The principles underlying the school's judiciary are discussed in detail in "On Law and Order" in this book.) The details of the system are, again, spelled out in the Law Book.

Despite the great variety of activities, and the full latitude and respect accorded to individual interests and rights, the school runs extremely smoothly. And despite the fact that, since the school's founding, the cost of living has gone up over threefold, the operating expenses of the school have not even doubled, thanks to the incredible -- and I mean incredible -- wisdom and frugality of the School Meeting.

Well, that's the thumbnail sketch I promised. If you've read this far, you know the basics of how the school works. Anything more, by way of detail or philosophical justification, you have to get by asking. We'll welcome the opportunity to talk with you.

When You Think of
the School Meeting,
What Passes Through Your Mind?
(A Former Student's Answer)

Laura Ransom

For me, the Sudbury Valley School Meeting had
one outstanding feature which sticks in my memory.
It was one of the rare settings in my life in
which my ideas were considered without regard to
my age, sex, relative experience or status in the
group. The concept of the School Meeting was to
"address one's remarks to the chair," depersonal-
izing them, focusing on content. While some found
this lacking in warmth, it meant that the ideas
were discussed with an absence of sexism or pat-
ronization. I rarely had the feeling of being
indulged, which, as a young woman, I had experienced so often. The structure demanded that the
ideas, motions and problems be confronted apart
from the personalities involved, a separation that
made possible the development of genuine political
equality. As has often been noted, this did not
mean that we came to the meetings all equally

prepared or educated or with the same influence on
each other. We came, thank goodness, some wiser
and some more foolish, some educated in the lessons of history and some wanting to live for the
moment. Some earned a respect which let them
present their intuitions, unsubstantiated, and
sway a vote, and some came with carefully reasoned
arguments and lost because they could not persuade
a majority that their cause was worthwhile. Political equality and fairly conducted meetings were
no insurance that we would be equally wise or
equally successful in convincing the School Meeting to do what we wanted. But we very clearly
were offered an equal chance, an equal opportunity.

The second point, and for me personally the
more important one, was that we had to give the
same opportunity to others. Some members of the
meeting spoke with eloquence and insight, others
were boring, obnoxious and rude. We had to listen
to them, too, if we wanted silence while we
spoke. Occasionally members presented the same
motions time and again, reintroducing ideas which
had been overwhelmingly rejected and stirring up
seemingly endless debate. They had a right to the
forum and to a vote on their ideas. On the more
serious side, some students and occasionally staff
engaged in obvious, direct, power plays challeng-
ing the School Meeting's authority. These chal-
lenges had to be countered. We had to attempt to
put aside our resentment at wasted meeting time,
or our perception of the aggressive intent of a
particular challenge and attempt to deal only with
the issues. Personal comment and directly addres-
sing other people in the room were out of order.

I personally sat on both sides of these
issues, as School Meeting member and as chairman
one year. I know it was an important experience

for me. I can say, however, that at the time I
little realized the exceptional situation in which
I was involved. I now realize that I have never
before or since earned the kind of equality and
power and respect that resulted. Then I was
mainly aware of the burden of being responsible
for the school and for my own corner of the community. Now I know that the investment was hardly
excessive in return for the rare opportunity to
participate in a community which offers equality
in its administration and in its daily life.

Five Myths about Democracy

Daniel Greenberg

"Democracy" seems to mean many things to many people. To the regimes of Eastern Europe it designates an autocratic one-party rule conducted for the presumed benefit of the masses; to the New Englander it designates universal suffrage in an open town meeting; to the Founding Fathers of this country it designated a complex system of representation and checks and balances. And so it goes. When the Sudbury Valley School was founded as a "democratic school" we naively thought that there would be widespread understanding of what this meant. It turned out that different people had quite different conceptions of what kind of institution a "democratic school" should be, and that even the members of the school community differed considerably on the question.

Does that imply that the word "democracy" is essentially meaningless, and that it cannot be used in ordinary conversation or written communication to convey a definite meaning? I do not think so. I think that there is, in fact, a core of meaning that this word conveys to all who use the English language discriminatingly, and that difficulties arise only through carelessness (or occasionally through conscious deceit). I think that for the most part our own problems with this word in the school arise from our failure to

explore its meaning in depth. As a result, we
have too often been satisfied with vague defini-
tions that missed the mark and led to controversy.

Instead of trying to refine our conception of
democracy by providing a definition of what it
means, I shall, in this paper, focus on several
things it does not mean. Over the years, it has
been possible to identify a number of recurring
errors that people in and out of the school have
been making when they observe our operation, or
engage in philosophical discussions. I shall
briefly identify five of these errors, in the hope
that their elimination will be a constructive step
toward the clarity we are seeking.

1. In a truly democratic school, everyone
will participate in decision-making processes.

People ask, "How many persons attend the
weekly School Meeting?" as if the important
criterion is the attendance level. This is the
Voter Participation mentality, that says that a
democracy requires full participation in the
voting process. In many countries there are laws
that require people to vote. The idea seems to be
two-fold: (1) the democracy isn't working if
everyone doesn't vote; and (2) the citizen who
doesn't vote is not a good citizen.

Both premises are wrong. Democracy rests on
universal suffrage, not on universal participation. What is essential is that each person have
access to a full share in decision-making.
Whether or not he uses that access is a private
matter, dependent on a variety of factors. As
long as there is true universal access, there is
true democracy.

Who actually participates in a given decision
is best left up to each individual. As soon as
the community forces persons to participate, it is

engaging in yet another "do-gooder" activity, like
forcing everybody to learn math, or to pray once a
day, or to do a good deed a day. Indeed, forcing
full participation is a singularly crude invasion
of the privacy of each voter: it signifies the
community's refusal to respect a person's decision
not to vote.

There are many reasons a person may choose
not to vote, and all are a priori just as valid as
a decision to vote. A person may feel that he is
not sufficiently well informed to express an
opinion on the issue at hand; in this case, forcing him to vote is a patent disservice to the community. A person may have more pressing business
elsewhere. A person may be more interested at the
moment in something entirely different; who are we
to say that his other interest, if pursued, will
be of less value to the community than his presence at the meeting or the poll? A person may
simply be content, on any particular issue, to
abide by the judgment of others -- a kind of
proxy, certainly a legitimate process.

There is no need to drag on with this catalogue of possibilities. The key idea is simple:
True democracy is universal suffrage, universal
access to the decision-making process; whether or
not a given person at a given time uses this
access is entirely a matter of his own private
concern, beyond the realm of public coercion or
public judgment.

2. In a truly democratic school, everyone
will take a full share in the daily round of
tasks.

People look at the distribution of administrative tasks in the school and ask, "What proportion of the school community takes an active role
in running the school?" as if the number of people

doing the administrative chores is the key factor.
This is the Community Service mentality, that says
that everyone ought to "do his share" in perform-
ing a certain list of routine services for the
community.

Again, this attitude is wide of the mark.
Democratic principles require that all persons
have an equal opportunity to take part in managing
community affairs. There must be no barriers of
sex, race, age, or of other such artificial and
accidental traits. The qualifications required
and duties expected for each position should be
clearly stated, and each position should be open
equally to all those who meet the qualifications
and seek to perform the duty. This is the basis
of the democratic election process, in which all
qualified persons who wish to be placed on the
ballot can have their names put in contention.
This is, of course, the way the school has always
operated.

Whether or not a given individual seeks to
take part in the daily administration is his own
private decision, based on many personal con-
siderations that the community is obligated to
respect. Forcing people to assume jobs they do
not want is a major invasion of privacy, and
should be done only in cases of extreme necessity
and demonstrated urgency. (One such instance in
our school is the Judicial Committee and the
reason this exception was made is a fascinating
chapter in the history of the school.)

The fact that, at any given time, only a
small number of persons wish to assume tasks that
are open to all should not be a matter of concern. Those who choose to abstain from administration may have a host of valid reasons for
abstaining. They may be no good at the work -- in
which case, forcing them to do it would be a real

disservice to the school. They may be focussed on
other things which will be of much greater service
to the school and the community than grudgingly
performed administration. They may find administrative tasks repulsive or offensive, in which
case forcing them to work would be a serious
invasion of their private world, implying that the
community has a right to force people to overcome
their private dislikes or objections. For example, I happen to think that for some time to
come, in the context of the current milieu, most
teenagers will find administrative tasks distasteful, and will avoid them at all costs, because
these tasks remind them of the kinds of services
they have been forced to perform against their
wills in nonschool situations. As a result, they
have come to abhor these tasks, and will avoid
them even when no coercion is involved. Of
course, there will always be exceptions, and hopefully in the not-too-distant future the exceptions
will become the rule.

I do not expect that there will ever be a
large percentage of people who will seek to participate in the school's administration, any more
than there will ever be a large percentage of
people who will seek to study music, or art, or
Latin, or physics. To see anything wrong with
this state of affairs is to take the point of
view, alien to our school's entire outlook, that
certain interests are in fact "good" and "important" for everyone to pursue. What is important,
and has been jealously protected at the school, is
the open access to all jobs and all pursuits, on a
regularly renewed basis.

3. In a truly democratic school, where all
are treated as equals, all will feel equal.

People ask, "Why does it seem that certain
segments of the school population feel inferior to
others, or are intimidated by others?" To begin
with, the very question itself is an unwarranted
invasion of privacy, and enters realms which we
have assiduously placed off-limits at the school.
As far as our democratic principles are concerned,
we have had to make sure that everyone, at every
time, and in every situation, is treated even-
handedly, with no trace of bias or prejudice of
any sort. That is a strong, specific statement of
aims, and it is one that we have been careful to
live by at all times.

We have never entered into the psyches of
School Meeting members, and I hope we never shall.
It takes no expertise in psychology to realize
that feelings of inadequacy, lack of self confidence, fear, self-deprecation, and other related
personality characteristics are not easy matters
to understand, and have roots in the full variety
of experiences that have impinged on a person in
his private life from the moment of birth onward.
To judge the democratic purity of a school -- or a
town -- by reference to the private psychological
worlds of its members is to confuse entirely the
private and the public.

People who suffer from psychological problems
must themselves be responsible for seeking a
remedy. The alternative is to have the community
feel responsible for assessing the psychological
health of each person, and for setting each person's house in order. I consider this alternative
a complete surrender of privacy, and I feel that
our country has already gone much too far in this
direction. Hopefully, the school will never opt
for this path, but will be content with constantly

reexamining itself to be sure that the school's
operations in no way introduce any objective
inequalities in the treatment of various persons.

4. <u>In a truly democratic school, where all
views are aired and debated, decisions will
finally be arrived at through consensus.</u>
People ask, "Isn't it a defect of the school
that you often have deep and sharp divisions
within you, and must often arrive at decisions
through a bitterly contested vote?" This attitude
reflects a view popular since the Enlightenment,
that in an environment of free exchange of ideas,
Reason should always guide us to the Best Solution. As applied to the school, the argument of
these critics is as follows: "If the school was
really as democratic as it claims to be, then all
controversies would receive a full, thorough, and
dispassionate airing, and in the end the view with
the greatest merit and good sense would prevail,
by consensus. The fact that the school often has
persistent divisions that must be decided by a
split vote shows that there is some defect in the
democratic process, so that instead of a free
airing of ideas, the school is merely getting a
power-play between factions."
This attitude, though especially popular in
these days of consensus, love, encounter groups,
team problem solving, etc., nevertheless is
essentially in error in its basic assumption that
calm reason produces a Best Solution for every
problem. In fact, only a minute number of essentially technical problems have a single best
solution. The more complex problems of everyday
living have a host of solutions, many of them
equally good alternatives backed by equally valid
arguments. Men of good faith, good intelligence,

and sound reason often differ profoundly on which
of these alternatives to pursue.

Indeed, the mark of a democracy is the
absence of consensus. Democratic procedure
implies that all the conflicting alternatives be
given a full and equal hearing, and be respected
and allowed to persist even when their proponents
are in the minority. In a democracy, consensus is
a rare and short-lived accident, as this country
found out in the 1960's. Repeated consensus is
always a symptom of powerful communal pressure to
force the dissenting minority to abandon its
position and accept the prevailing view.

For myself, I always heave a sigh of relief
when a hotly contested issue comes to the floor of
the School Meeting or the Assembly, because I see
in the very existence of such issues a reaffirma-
tion of our adherence to democratic processes.

5. In a truly democratic school, everyone
will be committed to defending the principles and
rights on which the school is based.

People say, "If yours is a truly democratic
school, every member of the school community would
be zealously committed to its survival. The
absence of universal commitment is a sign that the
school benefits a few people at the expense of the
majority." This is the Evangical viewpoint, that
if a person perceives the good, he must become
totally committed to it.

This attitude ignores both history and
psychology. There has never in history been a
situation where all -- or even a major proportion
-- of those who benefited from something have been
committed to its preservation. On the contrary,
our history books are one long chronicle of the
opposite thesis: that at any time, in any group,
only a small fraction of persons have been devoted

to protecting, maintaining, and furthering the
good things that the masses were enjoying.

Why this is so is a matter for social scientists to cope with, and is something that they
have not even begun to understand. Nor is it even
clear that we would ever want to have things
different. Often when we come across a community
that has a relatively large number of persons
committed to preserving its way of life -- for
example, the homogeneous religious communities of
past and present times -- we feel that they are
not of the character that we would prefer to see
in our own surroundings. Indeed, it can be argued
that the existence of a large mass of satisfied
citizens who are not wholly committed to the
struggle to preserve what they have is a necessary
counterweight to the small number who are committed. Perhaps the satisfied but seemingly indif-
ferent masses are a healthy reminder to all
concerned that there exist important things in
life other than the ideals to which the few are
committed. In this way, perspective can be maintained even while a struggle is being waged.

Five myths -- and there are many more.
Perhaps if we begin by adequately appreciating the
errors of these five, to which so many of us have
ourselves fallen prey from time to time, we will
be better equipped to deal effectively with other
similar errors that perplex us regularly.

Subtleties
of a Democratic School

Daniel Greenberg

Certain nuances in the operation of the school have emerged during the years we have been in existence that turn out to be very important in defining the school. A while ago someone gave me a book to read about an alternative school that appeared to him to be very similar to Sudbury Valley. I read the material I had been given, and my first reaction was one of horror, because I found the school described in the book so very different from us that I could not imagine how the person who gave it to me had ever though it was similar. Determined to get to the bottom of the matter, I reread the book and then the answer came to me. So much of the terminology was similar to the terminology that we use, that if you didn't have experience in understanding the subtleties of our school, you could easily get fooled into thinking that the other school was the same. The language was similar; the vocabulary was similar. It took very close reading to see how fundamentally different the two schools were. The more I thought about it the more I became convinced that this whole question is tied up with enrollment too, because I think that the better we are

recognized for what we are, the more likely it is
that the people who enroll here will really want
what we are offering.

One of the key strengths of our school is
that it related in a very profound way to American
tradition and experience. In The Crisis in
American Education (Sudbury Valley School Press;
Framingham, MA) we talk about this in general
terms, but I think there is a lot more to be said
on that subject. In many subtle ways this school
tunes in on deep elements of the American spirit.
This is a source of real strength for us, because
it links us intimately with the fate and future of
the country as a whole.

I have five items to discuss. In each case,
I will define the item, tell why I think it is
important to our school, and then compare the
situation in other schools.

Item 1: Political Neutrality

Ours is an apolitical school. It is a school
in which we consciously do not pay attention to
the political views of the people who seek to
become members of the community, where by "political" I mean the standard sense of the term, in its
broadest implication. We don't ask about party
affiliations, about philosophy, about class, about
any of the features that separate political factions in a society. We don't ask about these
things, we don't test for them in an indirect way,
we don't try to find out about them in a back-
-handed manner. In addition, we don't allow
political activity to take place on the campus.
In plain language, we don't allow the school in
any way to become involved in political activities
in the community.

Our rigorous political neutrality has been put to the test many times. For example, in the beginning, when we first opened, it was simply assumed by members of the so-called "Movement" that we were another "Movement" institution. If we happened to encounter anybody who was involved in the Movement, we would be greeted as "brothers." We would be asked such things as, "When are you planning to have your next rally?" We were approached by people in the community to use the building in support of an election campaign. It was assumed that any "brother" from any part of the country could come and camp out at the school. This was a widespread assumption. When it became clear that regardless of the private political views of the people concerned with the school, the school itself was going to maintain an absolutely rigid political neutrality from the beginning -- and this became clear very quickly -- we came to be considered enemies of the Movement, and in the Movement literature we were singled out for special ridicule and contempt for our non-political behavior. Finally, we were simply eliminated from the Movement literature. Unfortunately there was a spill-over to the community at large. I think that a lot of the parents in '68 had heard about the school through political connections, and they made the same assumptions. I think that contributed to some of our problems that year, when they found out that we weren't what they expected.

We had other tests of our political neutrality. For example, there were many times when students (it was particularly students, because I think the staff had worked this out, and understood it very well) wanted to have some kind of participation in peace rallies in '68 and thought the school should be involved. Later, there was "Moratorium Day" in October 1969. There was a

certain amount of discussion on whether the school
should be closed, because everybody was closing.
In this connection, it was instructive to see how
quickly the concept of political neutrality came
to be accepted here. It was really extremely
interesting to see that the strongest activists,
the people who felt most strongly about their
views, simply dropped any attempt to politicize
the school, and their arms didn't have to be
twisted in any way. They really accepted it once
it was explained to them.

Why is it so important? And why did they
realize it was important? The reason is embedded
deep in the American political spirit, in the idea
that people of divergent political and social
views can work together in a common enterprise
where they have common goals other than politics.
This is a deep and uniquely American idea. You
don't have to see eye to eye with all your co-
workers in order to create a valid enterprise. To
be sure, where political issues are concerned, you
can seek out your political friends and fight with
your political enemies. But an extremely important tradition in this country is that when other
matters of concern are at hand, other things that
are not inherently political by nature, you don't
pay attention to political differences; all people
can join hands in the enterprise. This feature
was built into the public school system here, a
system of education that is an original American
conception. One of the cardinal features of our
public schools was that all people, belonging to
all religions, having all political views, coming
from all classes of society, would come together
for the educational enterprise. In its essence,
education was a search for knowledge, and any view
was to be subjected to scrutiny.

That's the ideal. It may not always have
turned out that way in practice. But I don't
think it is too important to look at the defects
of the American public school system in practice,
for the purposes of this discussion. I think the
ideal is really clear; it is spelled out over and
over again in the American public school literature. The tradition of public education is that
in such a noble enterprise as the search for
knowledge, truth, enlightenment, everybody can
work together.

I do believe very strongly that this is an
important feature of our school. Anyone who knows
personally some of the people associated with the
school knows that the school community spans an
extraordinary divergence of political views, and
this has not been a barrier to working together.
The main point is that nobody need feel uncomfort-
able in the school, regardless of his political
views. Everyone has full freedom to express his
views and to hear others, and no one is ever made
to feel "square" or an outsider because he holds
views that may be in a minority on the political
scene.

As I just said, the public school system is
closest to us in this respect. By contrast,
alternative schools -- the so-called "free
schools" -- are virtually all identified with
specific political movements. Every alternative
school that I know about has stressed the political nature of its program. Sometimes this may not
be evident because of their use of language.
"Politics" has become a dirty word, and so it has
become very modish to hide the fact that what they
are doing is political. They prefer to call
themselves non-political even when they are doing
political things, and as a result it becomes hard
to spot the politics in their literature.

I think you will find time and time again that groups will try to hide the political nature of what they are doing by couching their work in moral terms, by referring to grander over-arching aims that don't show the political reality that they really are. That's why when you read the literature of an alternative school you have to read it carefully.

For example, you may find a school catalog that doesn't have a single word about politics in it, but you find that the things they stress are ecology, organic foods, a certain approach to the body, a certain approach to the sexes, towards family life -- all of the things that virtually constitute a political program for the organization of a community and a way of life. Their little brochures can be three pages long, but that is long enough for you to find out that their school is being set up by a group with a very focussed political program -- even though the word "politics" never appears. And of course the "insiders" know it. It's only the casual readers who are duped. It's like a code. Often they come here on a visitor's day and one of the first things they ask is, "How many people do you get studying ecology?" That's a code word -- they're not really interested in our curriculum, but they want to identify quickly whether we are "with it" or not.

Some schools are more overt, and say point blank that they are interested in people having certain specific political views, and that they carefully screen applicants and staff members to make sure they get politically pure people in their community. They say it in so many words. But for the most part, this is pretty well camouflaged in the literature of alternative schools, and you can pick it up only by reading carefully

and asking yourself, "Is this literature a code
for a certain community structure that these
people are advocating or isn't it?" Put our literature to that test, and you will see that it is
all clearly politically neutral. You simply
cannot put your finger on a program of specific
community action in our school writings.

So probably the most blatant difference
between our school and alternative schools started
by other groups is that the alternative schools
are virtually all connected to some political
movement. You should not take what I am saying to
be antagonistic towards other alternative schools.
I'm simply trying to point out a difference. I
think it is perfectly legitimate for any group to
set up its own educational institution if it wants
to. I'm not at all opposed to that idea; in fact,
I think it is part of our pluralistic scene. I
think political schools play the same role in the
political sector as parochial schools play in the
religious sector. There is nothing wrong with the
idea that people who have strong religious convictions should want to set up a school where those
convictions dominate. I don't have anything
against any group, right, left, or center, saying
they would like a politically pure school because
they have an ideal they want to nurture in a pure
environment. My only concern is to make sure that
people understand what they are going into; that
people don't think they are getting one thing when
they are in fact getting another. We don't want
people coming to this school thinking it is a
"Movement" school and then be disappointed that we
let in all these "right-wing creeps." And I don't
want people going to an alternative school thinking they are in an apolitical situation, when in
fact they are getting indoctrinated, which I think
happens much of the time.

Item 2:   The Existence of Rules of Order

      We have always thought it important to have official meetings of any group in the school operate according to some set of explicit, formal procedures. I don't attach any importance to Robert's Rules in particular. It makes no difference if they are Robert's Rules, Congressional Rules, Sudbury Valley Rules or any other set of rules. What is important is that we've always run our meetings according to strict rules of order.

      This contrasts to the usual way meetings are held, where somebody runs the meeting; I call that authoritarian model, and I think that is the most prevalent model. Somebody determines what is going to be discussed, who will talk when, when the discussion will be terminated, and how the decision will be made -- if he doesn't make the decision himself. This is the standard pattern of faculty meetings, religious groups, and so forth. There is somebody with power who does things in the way he thinks is right. Every now and then a person may complain, and some compromises may be made, but that's the way it runs.

      A second model that has become more avant-garde today, more "with it," more accepted by the "in" groups, is the extreme opposite of the authoritarian model, but similar to it in essence. This model is dominated by the mood of the group rather than the mood of an authority figure. It's a group meeting, a "togetherness" experience. The idea is that everything should be done by consensus: "We will all get together, and as long as there is disagreement, we are going to talk it over, to get a real meeting of minds, until we are all really together." The idea is the same as the authoritarian model in essence, because it's

governed by an arbitrariness, except that this is
the arbitrariness of the whole group spirit rather
than of an individual. There doesn't necessarily
have to be continuity from one day to another, or
from one hour to another; it is something that is
governed by the spirit of the occasion. Generally
speaking, ever since the encounter-group mania
that swept the country in the mid-sixties, it has
become very "in" to think that it's a good thing
to have meetings run that way, by group consensus,
better than having one authority run it. I don't
really know why this has happened. I think I
would personally ascribe it to the general decline
of individualism in this country, to the flight
from individual expression and strength and
submergence in a group as a substitute. This
approach has taken hold all over, even in corporations, where you would never have expected it.
They don't make decisions the way they used to;
instead, they get people together out in the
country for a few days, and give them some sort of
tremendous experience, the idea being that a
strong bond will be formed that will become the
basis for making decisions.

Both the authoritarian types and the group
types view the kinds of meetings we have in the
Sudbury Valley School with disdain. The idea that
decisionmaking should take place according to some
formal set of explicit procedures is repugnant to
both sides. The reason this is so is related to
what we talked about in item #1. The chief function of rules of order is to protect all views and
to give them as detached and thorough an airing as
possible. Rules constitute the main protection
for reason, intellect, objectivity, and detachment
in a group context, as opposed to feeling and
emotion. This is because rules ritualize the
equality of all views and all people. They are

set up specifically to equalize any view; they
make it possible for anybody to use the meeting,
to introduce a motion, to get the floor. They
protect a speaker from being shouted down, they
prevent an outburst of emotion on the floor, they
protect a debate, they prevent a personal argument
between two people that will bring out emotional
antagonisms rather than reasoned arguments.
That's their chief aim. As with every other aim,
you don't always succeed in attaining it. There
is always a way to violate the spirit of the
rules. Nothing on paper ever protects you totally. So some views can be shut out eventually if
they get on people's nerves enough. There is no
absolute protection. But the trend is unmistak-
able: to guarantee the rule of reason through
rules of order. This is why this item is related
to the previous one. In a situation where you are
looking for political sameness, there is nothing
more repugnant than a minority view; that's just a
pain in the neck. Wherever one wants ideological
purity, one doesn't want to guarantee equal exposure to all views. But in an apolitical institution like this school, such protection has become
important to us.

    That's why rules of order have survived
repeated onslaughts in the school. No sooner were
rules of order announced and they were attacked in
the summer of '68, and often again in the fall of
'68. People complained bitterly about the formality of the School Meeting. A good deal later
there was again a feeling of dissatisfaction about
the way the School Meeting was run -- dissatisfaction that again focussed on the formality of the
rules; and we actually set up a special committee
to study the functions of the School Meeting and
make recommendations for changes. Anybody who had
complaints about the School Meeting could come

forward; and there were some changes made in the
procedure as a result of this committee's work.
But the basic form was preserved, even though
there were certain people who felt that we just
shouldn't have rules, that people should be able
to say whatever they wanted, and we should be able
to make major decisions right on the floor. Earlier in '68 they said it a little more bluntly --
that the meeting should be a "happening." But in
fact the school's basic attitude toward rules of
order has been reaffirmed over and over again by
an overwhelming majority of the School Meeting
membership, until by now it is not an issue at
all.

In fact, the more people have come to realize
the significance of their rules, the more they
have taken advantage of them. The School Meeting
Record will show, for example, that as time has
passed a greater diversity of people introduce
motions. More people are coming to feel that they
have access to the political process. It is the
existence of a clear, explicit procedure that
protects and encourages them in doing this. You
can see it when you talk to students at the
school, even the littlest kids: "We want to have a
field trip and we have to go to the School Meeting
and introduce a motion for it." It's a beautiful
equalizer. They don't say, "We have to ask staff
member A to arrange it for us." They don't look
to an authority, and they don't say, "We have to
get everybody in the school community to agree
that it is a good thing." They realize that the
way the procedures are set up in the school, every
citizen of the school community has equal access
in presenting what he wants to the source of
power, the democratic School Meeting. Anybody who
has been at a School Meeting cannot fail to notice
that political "power blocks" use this access

regularly. A block will show up when something of
special interest is on the floor. A group of
people troops in for a motion, and troops out
later; all ages, not necessarily little or middle
or anything, but very well focussed, knowing
exactly what they are doing.

I think it is perfectly self-evident how this
fits into the American tradition. The establishment of rules was a very conscious effort on the
part of the founders of the country when they set
up the first legislatures, both in the states and
in the federal government. We have records of
debates and discussions on the rules of order in
Congress, and on the functions that these were to
serve -- in particular, to protect the rational
quality of the discussion.

I think you'll find this concept missing from
most other schools. Traditional schools are
almost totally run on the authoritarian model.
Alternative schools, interestingly enough, are
about equally divided. Many are run by a charis-
matic leading figure. Others are run as a continuing encounter group. I wouldn't be surprised if
this single feature alone accounts for the high
failure rate of so many alternative schools. They
just didn't have good procedures for making
decisions. They didn't have the decision-making
capability to air all the views and consider all
the options necessary to their survival. So when
the crunch came, they just gave up the ghost.

Item 3: The Rule of Law

This resembles the previous item in many
respects. By "rule of law" I mean the existence
of explicit, published rules governing the community, and the existence of a rational means for

arriving at such rules. The previous item was
limited to the procedures of the governing body;
this item refers to the actual laws governing
individuals and the community as a whole. Con-
ceptually, there is much in common between items
#2 and #3.

The rule of law is generally acknowledged to
be a cornerstone of orderly, organized society.
In our school, laws are always promulgated in
writing, and careful records are kept of the body
of precedents surrounding each rule. There is a
simple process for the adoption of new laws and
repeal of old, obsolete laws -- a democratic process accessible to all members of the community.
There is no opening, however small, for arbitrary
or capricious authority to step in.

The public schools remain one of the last
bastions of autocratic rule in our society. Power
generally resides in the principal, sometimes
elsewhere; it is not important to locate where it
is, only to note its autocratic nature. There is
in fact no rule of law. It is interesting how the
public schools have become sensitive to this
defect. There is a lot of agitation on the part
of various community groups to institute in public
schools some of the protections afforded by rule
of law. Usually, the schools respond by starting
to promulgate sets of rules and regulations, to
give the appearance that they're acceding to this
demand. This process first started in higher
education in the late sixties, and has slowly
filtered its way down to the high schools, but
rarely lower. What I find so fundamentally
dangerous about this trend is that it is basically
a fraud, because at no time does the absolute
source of power give up its right to change the
rules at will. The rules that hold today can be
replaced by a new set tomorrow. The community is

getting the external impression that there is a
clear set of fair rules, whereas in fact the real
power remains where it was before. I guess there
are always some people who will say that this is a
step in the right direction, but I've always felt
that in a situation like this the "step in the
right direction" is in fact a step in the wrong
direction, because it is meant to pull the wool
over the eyes of the public and make them think
there is real protection, in order to deflect
criticism.

What is perhaps more surprising is that, by
and large, alternative schools do not believe in
the rule of law either. They too operate in an
atmosphere of arbitrary rules that usually emanate
not from a single power figure, like a principal,
but from some rule-making body operating without
regular rules of order (see item #2). There is a
constant shifting of sands in these alternative
schools, depending on the mood of the population
each week.

We had tremendous pressure on us in the summer of '68 when we first opened, not to codify our
rules, since "next week we could get together and
change them," as many people said. These were
real issues in the school; there were groups who
argued vehemently that we shouldn't have written
rules. "We want to be able to modify things as
the spirit moves us." The first time we mimeo-
graphed a collection of the rules passed by the
School Meeting was at the end of August 1968, and
that very act of mimeographing was a stand on this
issue. It meant that a code of law was being
developed, and it also meant that we considered
the School Meeting to be a continuing legislative
body, so that we didn't have to start all over
making new rules each year. The promulgation of
the August 1968 code of School Meeting Resolutions

meant that the results of the summer of '68 were
not going to be for the summer only, but for the
future as well, until duly modified.

In alternative schools, power resides in the
momentary whim of the majority at a given instant.
This is part of a conscious effort by the majority
to make sure that the minority will always shift
with the majority. Alternative schools are often
open about this; they want to submerge the individuality of each member in the community. This is
usually explicit in the literature of these
schools -- that they hold the unity of the community to be of prime value and to take precedence
over everything else. So they will usually under-
mine any attempt to institute the rule of law,
since that would tend to make an individual feel
secure and protect him when he chooses to stand
apart.

Item 4: Universal Suffrage

This is the idea that everybody, every
citizen has a vote. It is really a simple idea.
The American experience has been an inexorable
march toward universal suffrage, which hasn't
stopped yet. This has been a root trend in
American democracy. In the early days, voting
used to be subject to all sorts of race and
property and age requirements. Slowly, unproper-
tied males, then blacks, then the females were
added, and recently the age has been reduced to
eighteen. It's just a matter of time before
people start asking why it shouldn't be sixteen or
lower. It is clear that there is a constant movement in the direction of universality.

There is a real difference between a democratic society that believes in universal suffrage
and one that doesn't. This difference reflects

itself in the whole society in all of its functions. For example, Athenian society was a pure
democracy for Athenian male freemen, of whom there
were several thousand; and it was based on a large
substructure of enslaved subjugated peoples and
also on a smaller substratum of women, who were
not slaves, but were second class citizens. Don't
think there was anything unstable about this. It
was quite stable, it lasted a long time. The only
reason this ever went under, really, was because
there were stronger empires around who defeated
the Athenians at war; but as far as their internal
structure was concerned, it was quite stable. The
fact that there wasn't universal suffrage meant
that elitism was an inherent part of the Athenian
world view, which held that there was a privileged
segment of society, and the rest of society was
there to serve them. This went to the heart of
the Greek world view, as can be seen, for example,
in Plato and Aristotle. Even after Greek democracy disappeared, that idea remained part of Western culture right up to modern times. Elitism
allows for democracy within the privileged group,
but this doesn't do any good for the rest of the
citizens. I think this trend of privileged democracy, which is so different from the egalitarian-
ism of universal suffrage, is evident right up to
the present day. Communist countries often use
the word "democracy" honestly, reflecting a
genuine belief that there ought to be democratic
procedures within an elite -- which in their case
is the party, the political elite of the proletar-
iat. What I am saying is simply that they do use
the word "democratic" in a sense that has a long
history in our culture. The American idea, by
contrast, is egalitarian.

      Universal suffrage was built into the school
from the beginning. We always felt that every

single person who is part of the community has to
have a say in it one way or another. We changed
our views on exactly how much of a say any segment
should have, and exactly where this should be
expressed. Much depended on how much we felt we
could get away with. In the beginning, we didn't
think we could get away with the School Meeting
making financial decisions, because our legal
advisors worried that such an arrangement wouldn't
stand up contractually in court. But the trend in
school was always clear. Our view was always that
everybody in the school, aged four and up, should
have an equal access to power. Many years ago, we
reached that state.

If we contrast the situation in other
schools, we see again that there have been interesting trends at various levels towards extending
the suffrage to a certain extent. But if we look
closely, we will see the true state of affairs
more clearly. Let's focus briefly on higher education, which I think is the best example. There
was a tremendous amount of hoopla in higher education, especially back in the sixties, about democ-
ratizing the universities. This was part of the
agitation on campuses. There was much talk of
spreading the decision-making power. But when it
was all over, who got any real new power? The
answer is only the faculty. In no case that I
know of did any real power go to the students.
Even when students were put on Boards of Trustees,
the number allowed to serve was strictly limited.
Imagine if we had in our by-laws that there should
be 15 trustees, of whom no more than three should
be students, no more than three parents, etc.,
etc., and you'll see the contrast right away. Our
Board of Trustees is a board of Assembly members,
period; anybody can become a trustee. We can have
an entire Board of outsiders, or of staff members,

or students, or anything. Whereas in the universities they made it look like they were doing
something to distribute the power, but they really
were going to keep it where it was all along. I'm
not saying there was no concession made. Real
concessions were made within the elite, to the
faculty. This is just what I'm talking about,
that the idea of democracy as it is sold in Acade-
mia, in the heart of our educational system, is a
Greek one: democracy is for the privileged. Time
and time again, if you talk to faculty members,
they'll confuse the issues very nicely. They'll
say, "There is no equality in real life. I know
more about biology than my students. I know more,
and I should have more to say about it." And they
say this quickly so nobody should see that they're
confusing the issue of subject matter with the
issue of political power, which of course are two
very different issues. The contrast to our school
is instructive.

Item 5: Protecting the Rights of Individuals

This school has a strong tradition that there
exist rights belonging to every individual member
of the school community, and that these have to be
protected in every way possible. For example,
consider the right of privacy. This right is not
something you can codify legally, it's not a rule
that has been passed; it is just something inherent in the school. It is one of the individual
rights we protect in this school. Because of this
right we do not have any kind of intervention in
the private affairs of students -- intervention
that characterizes other schools. There isn't
anything against it in our by-laws or rules, it's
just part of our tradition to shy away from that
kind of activity. If we do intervene, there is an

enormous burden on the school to justify it, before we can do it.

The idea of protecting the rights of individuals is an essential part of American culture. This is not an absolute concept; it's a much more subtle one, that involves a great deal of judgment. Which rights, how far they go, where the boundary line is drawn between individual and community, these are all things that have to be decided and worried about day in, day out, year in, year out. That's why this idea is on my list of subtleties, because it's not something where you just draw a line and say, "These are absolute rights." Where the line is drawn between community interest and private interest is a matter of constant judgment.

The vast majority of national experiences in the history of man have not recognized the idea of individual rights as paramount in importance. Wherever the transition from a loose family or tribal units to national units took place, it involved a tremendous shifting of emphasis to the group, an emphasis which had to put an enormous value on the group in order to keep it together. There is nothing "natural" about forming a nation. Perhaps there is something natural about forming small groups, but a nation is a large conglomerate that does not hold together simply by blood ties or by friendship; it is held together by some sort of Idea, and apparently the only way this can happen is through tremendous pressure on the individuals in a nation to give up their individuality and subject themselves to the Idea. So that formation of nations and states required shifting values towards community, and this went far towards downgrading the idea of the individual.

Contrast that with what went on in this
country in the late '60's and early '70's, a
situation which is inconceivable in any setting
other than the American one. It is simply stag-
gering that you can have a country at war, and
right through that war people will go on with
significant protests that are demoralizing and
disruptive -- and be protected by the courts and
legislatures and even by the government they are
attacking. Even in the worst crises, we have
hardly ever sacrificed our individual rights. For
exceptions, one has to think back to a "horrible
autocrat" like Abraham Lincoln . . . who abol-
ished the habeus corpus during the Civil War!
Even during the Second World War, when a tremendous panic and sense of insecurity swept the
country because we were totally unprepared for any
sort of military struggle, the internment of the
Japanese on the West Coast raised a tremendous
uproar of protest. The American attitude towards
individual rights has no parallel in history.
Which rights are protected, and how far, all this
is subject to debate; but the fact that they exist
and are worthy of protection is a sacred prin-
ciple.
     A democratic school that is rooted in the
American tradition has to have that feature too.
It is not necessary for me to talk about other
schools at length, because the rights of people in
schools are just simply not respected, even if
there is occasional lip service paid to this. In
public schools, this is true for teachers and
administrators, as well as being true -- and
well-known -- for students. Furthermore, the idea
of individual rights is absent from alternative
schools for reasons that I have spelled out
several times, because alternative schools are
primarily committed to the community idea.

Five subtleties, all essential to defining the particular character of the Sudbury Valley School, and marking clearly its place in the history of the American Experience.

Teaching Justice Through Experience

Daniel Greenberg

One of the most difficult ideas to convey to children is that of justice, as reflected in the social order. The concept itself is complex and multi-leveled. It has to do with the development of fair rules of behavior for human interaction; with the interpretation of these rules in the context of daily life; with the acculturation of new members of the community to these rules; and with the fair monitoring and enforcement of these rules. Each of these aspects involves a great deal of human wisdom and judgment, much of which comes only through accumulated experience.

At first blush, the task of teaching justice to a new generation of youngsters seems forbidding. And indeed, viewed as an exercise in teaching moral philosophy, the task is virtually unattainable, as every moral preacher in history has found out. You can't just talk at people about good and evil, right and wrong, and hope to affect their actions. The reason is simple: if the hearers are young and inexperienced, such talk is boring and relates to nothing they can lay their hands on. If the hearers are older, they are usually set in their ways and unaffected by mere talk.

The challenge is this: how do you teach a socially acceptable concept of justice to children in a way that will acculturate them, interest them, involve them, and affect their future behavior? The answer lies in two words: <u>through experience</u>. Let's take a closer look at how this is done.

Consider the first aspect of justice, the development of rules governing human interactions in the community. In our society, we expect these rules to emanate from the community, in what we call a "democratic process" of legislation. Western democracies are based, among other things, on the belief that regulations made with the participation of all affected members of the society have a better chance of being valid, and of being <u>considered</u> valid by the affected parties.

The chief non-family social setting of children in developed societies is the school. What better place to begin to give children the experience of democratic rule making, with all the trappings? Where better to learn the art of debate, the need for taking other people's views into account, the benefits of open-mindedness, the balancing forces of personal and community interests, the nature of political power-blocs, the joy of victory and the anguish of defeat, the ability to recoup a loss and plan for future gain?

It would seem almost essential to begin teaching children in the real context of their early social setting, the school. Yet, this is almost never done. Small wonder that we hear on all sides a litany of complaints about adolescent lawlessness and indifference to community welfare.

Consider another aspect of justice, law enforcement. In our type of society, we hold law

enforcement to be a product of the democratic
order, engaged in by public servants chosen directly or indirectly by the people and accountable
to the people. We hold trials before our peers,
and accept judgment from our equals. Again, the
idea is that the fairest and most acceptable form
of enforcement in a free democratic society is one
that involves the whole community on an equal
footing.

Here, too, the place children have for
developing their sense of justice is the school,
where they spend a dozen or more of their formative years sheltered from the outside world, held
tightly in their own child-centered world. What
could be more important to their future behavior
in adult society than to develop, through experience, an understanding of the subtleties of law
enforcement? How enriching it is to deal directly
with the evaluation of evidence, the consideration
of extenuating circumstances, and the careful
balancing of such ideas as prevention, deterrence,
vengeance and rehabilitation.

Our school has, for nineteen years, laid
great emphasis on the development of a sense of
justice in children through direct experience.
From the beginning, we have operated along lines
that parallel the realities of adult experience in
the surrounding community. All rules, without exception, are created by a legislative body called
the School Meeting, modeled on the New England
Town Meeting, at which every student and every
teacher has one (and only one) vote. No hidden
powers of any kind whatsoever are reserved to some
higher authority. The School Meeting reigns supreme and students age 4-19 experience at all times
the full challenge of creating and maintaining the
real social order that is this school. This is no
showpiece Student Assembly, or Mock Parliament.

This is the real thing, where real rules govern real behavior in the real life of the school.

Similarly, all law enforcement takes place through a judicial system established by the School Meeting in which everyone participates. Students are responsible for investigating infractions, for trying alleged rule-violators, and for deciding what to do with guilty parties.

The results of this remarkable system of justice are fascinating to observe. To begin with, the school is noticeably well-ordered, much to the surprise of many outsiders, who wonder at the deep sense of internal harmony present in a school where there is so much personal freedom in daily activities. There is virtually no vandalism, and little overtly destructive activity. School Meetings take place weekly, Judicial Committee meetings about three times a week. Rules are proposed, debated, voted on, revised and refined by the School Meeting, and enforced and interpreted by the Judicial Committee. All are published in a School Meeting Law Book given to everyone.

The judicial process is smooth. The Committee deliberations are as intricate as the cases before them; some brief, others lasting days.

The result is a student body that learns about justice through active participation in its definition and administration. Graduates go out into the world ready to take their place at once as responsible members of the community at large.

On Law and Order

Daniel Greenberg

The judicial system at Sudbury Valley is one
of the keystones of the school's structure, and
has long been our pride and joy. We have always
felt, based on the values of the American experience, that due process of law is an essential
element in a school embodying the principles of
personal liberty, mutual respect, and political
democracy. Early in the first year of the
school's existence, the School Meeting devoted
long hours to establishing the legal principles
and juridical structure of the school, with
results that quickly produced a stable social
order and a prevailing feeling among students,
staff, and parents that here everyone got a fair
shake when brought before the bar of justice.

The system which was created in 1968-69
continued unchanged for over a decade. It was
designed, as was so much else in the school, with
an eye toward the future, when we hoped to have a
student body of many hundreds (perhaps thousands). As the years passed, and it became clear
that our growth would be somewhat more gradual,
those aspects of the school that were more particularly suited to large communities were revised
one by one, to accommodate reality. Among the
systems that came under review and were modified
by the School Meeting was the judicial system.

The School Meeting felt that the original system was too cumbersome for a school community numbering no more than one hundred souls. The most serious problem with the old system (though not the only problem) was the length of time it took for a judicial matter to be settled. Barring some major crisis (of which there were a mere handful over the years), the shortest time required to resolve a judicial matter was three weeks, and the average time was more like four or five weeks. In the overwhelming majority of cases, the original incident had long been forgotten by all concerned. There seemed to be no way of shortening the time in the framework of the old system, or of resolving other problems with it. A new judicial system was carefully fashioned with the intention of eliminating the existing problems while preserving the good features that we wished to keep.

The judicial reform of 1979, which was centered around the creation of the Judicial Committee ("JC"), was greeted with enthusiasm by virtually all School Meeting members. For five years, it maintained the tradition of justice and fairness for which we have been widely known and praised. Many people labored hard, and with pride, to serve in the system in various capacities.

In 1984 the system was further refined. We have lived with the system long enough to understand it well; we can appreciate its strengths and spot its weaknesses. The system is working well. I would like to take an analytical look at what we have.

II

Before proceeding to the particular, some
discussion is in order about the general.

There are five distinct stages to the
judicial process. These are, in serial order:

1. <u>Allegation</u>. A person is alleged by someone to have committed a misdeed. In the world at
large, this allegation can be brought by private
individuals (by which I include groups, partner-
ships, corporations, committees, or other private-
ly organized entities) or by governmental agents.

2. <u>Investigation</u>. If the allegation is
considered to merit further action, an investigation is made of the circumstances surrounding the
allegation. In the outside world, the investigation can be carried out by the police, by members of the justice division of the government, or
by private individuals.

3. <u>Charge</u>. If the investigation is deemed
to have yielded sufficient cause for further
action, a charge is made that a specific law has
been violated, and the alleged violator is brought
to trial. The laws concerned may or may not be
written (statutes vs. common law) and the alleged
wrongdoings may lead to criminal trials or civil
suits. In the outside community, the charges can
be brought by individuals or by government officials, in the latter case usually by agents of one
or another department of justice.

4. <u>Trial</u>. Once a charge is made, the case
comes to trial. The trial must follow prescribed
rules of procedure that are known and considered
fair. In the community at large, the trial can be
held before a judge, with or without a jury, or
before an arbitration panel, with or without right
of appeal, depending on circumstances; usually,
however, there is some mechanism for appealing a

decision against a defendant. The trial delivers
as its culmination a verdict or decision. In our
system, there is no double jeopardy, which means
that a person found innocent of a particular
charge of wrongdoing may not again be brought to
trial on the same charge.

     5. Sentence. If a person is found through
the trial process to have done wrong, that person
is sentenced (by which I include, for purposes of
this discussion, civil decisions assessing
damages, penalties, etc.). In the world at large,
sentencing is usually carried out by a judge, most
often the trial judge, but occasionally by the
jury in certain types of jury trial. There is
always an opportunity to appeal a sentence on
certain specified grounds.

     The entire five stage process outlined ever
so briefly above constitutes the generally accepted juridical system in most societies. Where
societies differ radically from one another is in
the way these steps are carried out -- the "rules
of the game." In this country, we have laid great
stress on having the whole process take place
according to "due process of the law," a phrase
which over the years has come to be laden with
meaning for all Americans. Generally speaking,
"due process" assures each and every one of us
that we are to be given a fair shake at every one
of the five stages of the juridical process.
"Fair shake" is not, of course, any more specific
or enlightening than "due process" in and of
itself, but a great deal of legal history has
given rich content to these words, and most
citizens of this country, from all walks of life,
have a rather good idea of what they mean.

     Let's put it this way. We do not expect to
be subject to frivolous or trumped-up allegations. We expect investigations to be thorough

and complete, not whitewashed and not such as
fabricate "facts" or suppress truths. We expect
charges to be specific, relevant, and not ex post
facto. We expect trials to be open, fair, not
biased, and such as give full rights and oppor-
tunities to the accused to be adequately defen-
ded. And we expect sentences to be fair, and to
reflect in a balanced manner society's need for
rehabilitation, retribution, and prevention. Any
society that does not fulfill these expectations
in its legal system is considered by us to be
severely, fundamentally, flawed.

III

The original juridical system instituted in
Sudbury Valley by the School Meeting in 1968-69
dealt with each of the five stages in a methodical
way.

Allegations of wrongdoing by a member of the
community could only be made by individuals (or
groups, committees, or school corporations).
There has never been a School Meeting official who
was given the duty to bring allegations on behalf
of the school or any of its organs. The allegations were made either in writing, or orally, for
presentation to the Committee on School Affairs
("CSA"). (Making an allegation against someone
came to be called "bringing a person up." The
origins of this phrase are shrouded in mystery and
myth. None of us really remembers whence it came,
but the phrase has stuck to this day.)

The CSA was composed of persons picked by lot
from among the school population, distributed
evenly across all age groups. Service was required, meetings were held frequently, and the
term of service was for a period of one month.

Each newly chosen CSA elected a chairman to keep
things organized and moving. The CSA heard the
allegations, and decided whether they merited
investigation. If so, the CSA investigated as it
saw fit, calling witnesses, and having what
amounted to a subpoena power to require witnesses
to appear and testify. (If someone refused to
testify, the matter would be brought to the School
Meeting. No one, of course, was required to testify against themselves.) When CSA completed its
investigation, it filed with the School Meeting
(for publication in the weekly School Meeting
Record) its report of the facts of the incident,
as revealed by its investigation. The CSA made no
determination or charge relative to the breaking
of any rules. Its report was viewed solely and
entirely as an objective factual account of the
events that transpired around the allegation.

The School Meeting at its weekly session
received the CSA report. At that time, any School
Meeting member could, on the basis of the report,
press charges against an alleged violator. The
member pressing charges then became the prosecutor
at the subsequent trial (together with such help-
ers as that person chose to enlist). There was no
official school prosecutor, nor was the prosecutor
necessarily the person who made the original
allegation before the CSA. The charge had to
refer clearly to a specific rule that the prosecutor held to have been violated. At this juncture,
the School Meeting as a whole acted as a kind of
grand jury, voting either to permit or not to
permit the prosecutor to proceed to trial; the
School Meeting voted on the basis of the CSA
report -- that is, on the basis of the members'
perception that the CSA report gave sufficient
grounds to warrant a trial. That, and no more.

At this point, the Law Clerk entered the picture. The Law Clerk was a School Meeting official
elected to serve half a year, whose function it
was (much like the Clerk of the Court in the outside world) to keep clean, complete, and accurate
records of all court proceedings. The Clerk made
sure the trial was assigned a trial number; notified the defendant of the charge and of the trial;
and recorded the defendant's plea. If the plea
was "guilty," the trial was automatically ad-
journed and the process moved on to sentencing.
If the plea was "not guilty," the trial was set
for a specific day in the week following the
School Meeting's vote to allow a trial.

The trial procedure was formal and fixed,
spelled out in detail in the School Meeting Law
Book. The School Meeting Chairman presided, and
the defendant could either represent himself or
have someone help him with his defense. The jury,
six in number, consisted of disinterested volunteers (or, if necessary, dragooned "volunteers");
anyone with an interest in the outcome or prior
knowledge of the circumstances could not serve as
a juror. The trial was open to any School Meeting
members who wished to attend. The proceedings and
verdict were recorded by the Law Clerk.

If a guilty verdict was rendered, the School
Meeting proceeded to sentence the defendant. This
was done by the presentation of one or more sentence motions on the floor of the School Meeting,
each motion generally requiring two readings
before passage. Anyone could present a sentence
motion, but the actual sentence had to be decided
by the School Meeting as a whole.

IV

The judicial system just described was uni-
versally acknowledged to be fair, to protect all
the rights of the accused while serving fully the
interests of order in the school. It was, however, cumbersome, and took several weeks from the
first allegation, through CSA investigation and
report, through School Meeting motion for a trial,
through trial, and then through two readings of a
sentence.
    But the real problem lay in the simple fact
that the school was, and always has been, small.
Everyone knows everyone, people respect each
other, and everyone knows that they will be
treated fairly. This had an interesting effect on
the judicial process. As the years passed, and
confidence in the system and the school grew, the
number of cases that went to trial diminished and
then went to zero, and remained at zero year after
year. Plainly put, people did not press charges
unless the case was clear; and those charged,
knowing this, and accepting the fact that they
would be dealt with justly, always admitted their
guilt and "took their medicine." The system
worked so well that for the most part it didn't
have to work at all.
    From a practical vantage point, the investi-
gation served as the trial, because it was fair,
and the accused did not feel a need to go beyond
it.
    This central development is what led ulti-
mately to the thoroughgoing reform that brought
about the present juridical process. If the de
facto situation was that the CSA, as investigator,
was in effect trying the case and determining
guilt and innocence, why not admit this de jure?
And if the school community had such faith in the

CSA's fairness, why not let the entire process
take place there, from beginning to end?
    In this way, the Judicial Committee was born,
replacing the old CSA in form and in changed function. To take care of the new system, Judicial
Clerkships were created, replacing the Law Clerk,
and possessing new duties and responsibilities
appropriate to the role of the JC.

                          V

        Let us look closely at how the original JC
worked, from 1979 on. The committee itself was
made up of members picked by lot from the various
student age groups, to serve for two months; and a
staff member available to serve at the time the
Committee meets. The Committee was chaired by the
two Judicial Clerks, who served slightly more than
two months (four terms to a school year). In
addition to chairing the meetings, they were
responsible for record-keeping and, in general,
for the smooth operation of the judicial process
at school.
        The actual steps of the judicial process,
previously described, were all handled by the JC.
As before, all allegations of misdeeds were
brought to the JC by individuals, in writing.
(There were no longer provision for oral presentation of complaints.) The JC decided whether an
investigation was warranted, and, if so, proceeded. The first step was almost always --
except where physically impossible -- asking the
accused to plead to the charge. If the plea was
"guilty," the investigation was over, with the
account of the accuser being accepted by the
accused, and the guilt being admitted. If the
plea was "not guilty" -- as it not infrequently

was -- the investigation proceeded, supposedly in
the form of a mini-trial, until the JC finally
felt ready to render a verdict. The defendant had
the right, if found guilty, to appeal to the
School Meeting and ask for a full formal trial, in
the old format. (This right was never exercised.)

A guilty plea or verdict led to sentencing,
which took place immediately and was decided by
the JC. Sentences that were considered by the
defendant to be too harsh or unfair could be
appealed to the full School Meeting. Several such
appeals were made, some of which led to a modifi-
cation, not always in the direction the defendant
had in mind, by the School Meeting of the sentence
imposed by the JC.

The entire process, from complaint through
sentence (if guilty), could take as little as a
few hours. Rarely did it take more than a few
days. There was full opportunity for the accused
to appeal both the trial and the sentence; this
avenue of appeal was considered by the School
Meeting to be a safety valve that ensured fairness
and due process in the system as a whole, even
though several generally accepted aspects of due
process were missing from the abbreviated JC
procedure. The system worked smoothly, the various JC clerks were extremely careful, hardworking,
and fair-minded, and the general feeling at school
was that people continued to be, as they always
had been, treated with an exceptional degree of
fairness and justice.

VI

Still, there was a problem, one that was
subtle but slowly revealed itself in greater
clarity as the years went by. When the CSA system

was in force, fairness wasn't the only currency
held dear. The <u>forms</u> of justice and due process
were also carefully preserved. As students
entered the school and became acclimatized to its
environment, they developed a profound understanding of the American legal system and the great
constitutional, statutory, and customary rights
and safeguards that went into the meaning of due
process in our culture. This general awareness
was a constant feature of the school, year in,
year out.

With the substitution of the JC system, fairness and justice remained, but due process in its
ramifications slowly faded from view, until only a
few people at school had a clear notion of what it
means, or even thought that it had much to do with
the school. Thus, one of the greatest gifts we
bestowed on our students, an appreciation of their
legal rights and duties in our society, was no
longer among the legacies we gave them.

Indeed, as time went by, there were a few
disturbing signs here and there that the full
trappings of due process might not be excess
baggage even at Sudbury Valley. Minor irregulari-
ties in JC procedures -- none of which led to
known miscarriages of justice -- gave several
people pause to wonder whether we might not have
"thrown out the baby with the bathwater," and
perhaps opened the door to possible abuses, albeit
inadvertent, in the future.

As a result, a number of refinements were
introduced in 1985, designed to restore some of
the benefits that had fallen by the wayside.
Let's take a close look, step by step, at how the
Judicial System now works.

The school appears by now to have a well-
established tradition that all allegations of misdeeds be made by individuals, without the need for

any school officials to supplement this course.
This is as it has been from the beginning, and as
long as there is a full complement of socially
responsible people at school -- which, in effect,
is as long as the school will continue to function
according to its basic principles -- there does
not seem to be a reason to modify this approach.
For the sake of a clear record, all complaints are
written, and there are plenty of people around who
are glad to help the illiterate put into writing
their oral complaints, by serving as scribes and
assistants.

The next step is the crucial one. At the
time the complaint is presented, no one knows
whether it is serious or frivolous, whether it
does or does not involve a breach of the rules,
whether the alleged accused was or was not involved and, if so, whether alone or with others.
These uncertainties are the reason an investigation is needed, and the JC -- as did its prede-
cessor, the CSA -- carries out such an investigation (as its mandate expressly requires). But the
important point is that at this stage what we want
is a report on the facts; there is yet no concrete
charge, no trial, no plea.

Only when the JC has completed its investigation (and only if it has succeeded in finding out
something of substance) is a charge entertained,
by the JC itself. It is in the best possible
position to zero in on the exact violation that
appears to have been committed, and on the exact
parties involved. In a very real sense, the JC is
properly the school's grand jury, collecting all
the evidence, and then preparing charges for trial
where there is sufficient reason to proceed. And
the very constitution of the JC, being a cross-
section of the school, assures everyone of fair
treatment by their peers.

Once a charge has been made by the JC against someone, the wheels of due process can turn, and nothing is to stop them from turning smoothly and promptly. The JC clerk notifies the person charged, and a plea is entered. If "guilty," a trial is not needed, and sentence can be imposed.

If the plea is "not guilty," a trial must be held, the way they were held in the past. The trial is scheduled by the presiding officer, the School Meeting Chairman, within a day or two of the time when the defendant was notified and pleaded "not guilty;" six disinterested School Meeting members serve as jurors; the JC, as bringer of the charge, arranges for a prosecutor; the accused can defend himself or enlist assistance in the defense; and the trial is open to all School Meeting members, as it should be.

Sentencing is in the hands of the JC. In most cases, the investigation, charge, guilty plea and sentence take place in one continuous sequence, since the overwhelming number of infractions are of a nature where this can take place with no violence to justice. In the few complex cases, a little more time is needed; but the JC's involvement from beginning to end gives it a unique vantage point from which to come up with a fair sentence, and again its constitution as a cross-section of peers is a critical reassurance of fairness to all who come before it.

VII

When all is said and done, the above analysis reaffirms the essential soundness of the existing juridical process. By clearly separating investigation, charge, and trial, we make everyone aware of the need for clearly drawn charges, based on clearly promulgated rules; for full notification of each defendant as to precisely what they are accused of doing; for an impartial trial; for an opportunity to prepare the best defense available. In this way, due process is joined to fairness in the uniquely constituted judicial system of the school.

The Silent Factor

Hanna Greenberg

I would like to write briefly about a subject
that is almost never mentioned in Sudbury Valley
publications, for what I think are good reasons.
In fact, I am not quite sure it is wise to write
this little piece!

When the school was in a state of development
prior to opening and in the early years, we con-
centrated much of our thought on what can be best
called "children's rights" in a political social
sense. Our thinking as reflected in our writings
was focussed then on the structure of the school
as a democratic institution dedicated to allowing
children their full rights, which were daily
denied them in all other schools -- such as the
right to justice and equality under the law, as
well as the right to spend their time according to
their own wishes. We formulated our own set of
rules for behavior, binding on the whole community, children and adults alike. "A person
cannot infringe on another's rights." "A person
cannot disturb another's activities." "A person
cannot use another's private property without
permission." "A person cannot endanger the safety
of another." And so on in that vein. A judicial
system evolved to safeguard these rights and to
ensure fairness and justice.

In addition we organized the school to allow maximum freedom from adult interference in the daily lives of the students. As long as children do no harm to others, they can do whatever they want with their time at school. The adults in other schools plan a curriculum of study, teach the students the material and then test and grade their learning. The adults at SVS are the guardians of the children's freedom to pursue their own interests and to learn what they wished. They also are there to answer questions and to impart specific skills or knowledge when asked to by the students.

The structure of Sudbury Valley provides the foundation for a second aspect of the school that we usually don't say much about, but which is nevertheless one of the school's major features: creating and maintaining a nurturing environment in which children feel that they are cared for. From the beginning, we shied away from writing about the warm atmosphere that we created. I believe that we have been reticent about this aspect for many reasons, some of which I would like to go into here.

First and foremost, we operate under the assumption that if we ensure that justice and freedom will prevail, the students will thrive. They will feel safe and secure enough to develop their own character and to chart their own course through life in a healthy and exciting way, no matter what we do as adults, as long as we don't interfere.

Second, Sudbury Valley was set up to be a day school complimenting the child's family but never superceding it in importance. Thus the assumption is that the child receives a full measure of love from within the family, and uses the school to develop a wider range of relationships, from close

and intimate to very casual, all of course
determined by the children themselves.

Third, we always felt that while you can
legislate rights, you can't legislate feelings.
If an institution promises a democratic structure
and respect for children's rights, one can see
rather quickly whether it is delivering the goods.
But if it promises tender-loving-care, one can
never know what it truly means. So we never
talked about anything to do with feelings.

Fourth, schools in our culture are not
expected to provide a congenial environment for
internal growth. Their primary purpose is to
impart skills and knowledge and to prepare the
young for a successful career. At Sudbury Valley,
we want a place that does not rob children of
their time to explore and discover their inner
selves. So we have focussed in our writings on
the reality of the existing schools, and talked
about rights and freedom to do what you want with
your time, and we did not talk about more elusive
emotional matters which nontheles occupied a
major part of our day-to-day time and energy.

The ever-changing realm of personal growth is
too intangible and ephemeral to grasp with scientific precision. Like the beauty of nature, it is
evanescent and transitory. Artists endeavor to
capture the moment and immortalize it, but art at
its pinnacle is a poor approximation of what
nature can do. Because we can't quantify an experience we often seem to underestimate its importance. In our industrial-technological era, we
measure everything and reduce all complexities to
computerized data sheets. But life as it flows
will not be measured without losing its meaning.
The same is true with the children at our school
who don't come to take classes, but who come to

live their lives, to explore nature, themselves
and our culture. They experiment, observe, analyze and dream. They grow, mature and get themselves ready for adulthood. But the how and what
and why is each person's private affair and we do
not impinge on it in order to evaluate it. So we
cannot really explore or analyze or lay out for
all to see what I think is the most important
aspect of our school. We cannot even begin to
describe the way we nurture the growth; support
the kids when they feel lost or floundering;
reassure them and teach them that we believe in
them and that they can do anything they want to if
they work hard at achieving their goals.

Sudbury Valley is a complex community. Its
objectives and structure are clearly delineated
and articulated. But what makes it all work is
intangible and mysterious. It is made up of many
small actions, that together form a living and
ever-changing educational institution. It is a
place where the students can learn how to be
themselves -- with self-knowledge, with confidence, and with joy, strengthened by the knowledge
that the adults around them are committed to nurturing their growth.

"When You Were Young…"
A True Story

Daniel Greenberg

"Will you help us write a complaint?"

I was startled from a mid-day reverie as I sat on the couch outside the office. Standing over me, peering at me somewhat hesitantly, were Adrian (age 9) and Naomi (7). "Maybe we should find Marge."

I looked at them for a moment. "What for?" I asked. "Keith (13) and Patrick (8) were disrupting our activities in the quiet room," came the answer. Idly wondering whether I, in turn, should file a complaint against them for their activities in the quiet room, I answered, "Sure," and we marched into the empty office.

It was 1:30. Virtually all the staff was closeted in the newly refurbished stereo room, where they had been meeting with interested students since 11:00 to decide the future use of the room. My task at hand seemed trivial in comparison. Nevertheless, I sat at the office desk, pen in hand, looking as official as I could. Adrian stood close by my right, Naomi leaned over the edge of the desk to my left, both watching every move I made, every word I wrote. This was to be a serious enterprise.

Complaint form before me, I turned to Adrian and said, "Start at the beginning. The very beginning."

"I probably shouldn't have called them names," said Adrian, a bit worried. "That was probably wrong."

"Start from the beginning. What happened?"

"Adam (8) and I were playing in the barn alone. Keith and Patrick came in and started teasing Jeremy Rahn (12)."

"Jeremy Rahn was there too?" I asked.

"He came in. Then they came. I called them names to protect Jeremy Rahn. I did it to help him."

Wondering why Jeremy needed Adrian's protection, I asked him to go on with the story.

"Then they chased us. Keith took my hat, and we ran out of the barn. Joshua (7), Adam and I escaped."

"Joshua was there too?" I asked, rewriting the story yet another time.

"Jeremy, Patrick and Keith chased us. I got away, grabbed my hat, then Keith picked me up, dragged me back to the barn, but we escaped --."

"Just a minute," I interrupted, sensing that I was losing any semblance of understanding of what had taken place. "Why was Jeremy chasing you too, if you were protecting him?"

"I don't know," answered Adrian with a smile. By now the words were spilling out in an excited recitation. His eyes were glistening. There was no stopping him.

"Then we tried to run to the main building and they trapped Adam in the sports closet and Joshua ran and told me and I went to rescue Adam. I made believe I was helping them lock him in but I didn't really and he escaped and I was in but I got out --."

At this moment a happy and calm Adam walked into the office and stood by Naomi. He certainly didn't look to me like someone who had just endured a harrowing experience.

Adrian was really into it. I turned to him and asked, "Did you have a good time?" He laughed heartily. "Yes," he said. "How about you?" I asked Adam. "Yes. I don't want to write a complaint."

"But they disrupted our activity," Adrian protested.

"What activity?" I asked.

"The magic show."

I hadn't heard of any magic shows that day. Knowing I was letting myself in for it, I said innocently, "What magic show?"

"Naomi and Mindy's (7)," answered Adrian.

A cheerful Joshua had joined us by now. Naomi, who had been silently watchful throughout, perked up at the mention of her name. "We tried to kick them out of the room, but they wouldn't go," she said with excitement, "then we pushed them." "And I tried to get them to go," chimed in Adrian. Joshua was smiling. Adam was somber.

"Can I tear up the complaint?" Adam said.

Naomi grinned. Joshua smiled. I asked Adrian, "What would happen if the complaint remained?"

"They would stop doing it," he answered with a great show of confidence in the effectiveness of the school's judicial system.

"Do you want them to stop?" I asked.

"No," he answered with a hearty laugh.

Adam tore up the complaint. General satisfaction. Then Adrian turned to me as he was preparing to leave and, with a broad smile, asked me, "When you were young, did you have such adventures?"